A GUIDE TO LIFE

Jewish Laws and Customs of Mourning

A GUIDE TO LIFE

JEWISH LAWS

AND

CUSTOMS

OF

MOURNING

Rabbi H. Rabinowicz, B.A., Ph.D.

Minister, Dollis Hill Synagogue, London

With the Sanction of the former Chief Rabbi
The Very Rev. Dr. Israel Brodie

KTAV PUBLISHING HOUSE, INC.

New York

Library of Congress Cat. No.: 67–19371

First published by
Jewish Chronicle Publications
25, Furnival Street London EC 4

© Rabbi Dr. H. Rabinowicz 1964

9-88

This edition
Published 1967 by
KTAV Publishing House
120 East Broadway
New York, N.Y. 10002

Printed in Great Britain

CONTENTS

I am indebted to MR. MAX SLESS, who wishes to dedicate this work to the memory of

EVA ROSALIND SCHER

She died young, in very tragic circumstances.

Sincere, pious, upright and faithful.

SCHEME OF TRANSLITERATION

(For Memorial Prayers)

The following equivalents in transliteration have been used throughout this book.

Beth with dagesh is ... B	Lamed L
Beth without dagesh is V	Mem ... ... M
Gimmel ... ... G	Nun ... ... N
Daleth with a dagesh is DD	Samekh ... ... S
Daleth without dagesh is D	Pe with a dagesh ... P
HE ... ... H	Pe without dagesh ... F
Wav V	Tsadek ... ... Ts
Zayin ... ... Z	Koph ... ... K
Heth ... ... CH	Resh ... ... R
Teth ... ... T	Shin ... ... SH
Yod ... ... Y	Sin ... ... S
Kaph with dagesh is ... K	Tav ... ... T
Kaph without dagesh is CH	Tav without a dagesh ... S

INTRODUCTION

JUDAISM, we are constantly reminded, is more than a creed; it is a way of life. Its doctrines and teachings are given practical expression in our daily actions, so that the difficult journey through life is eased and ennobled. Our Sages emphasise that it is the sacred duty of the Jew so to conduct his life as to make it a continuous act of service to God and to man.

The real purpose of religion is to open the heart to true joy and to strengthen the spirit in those inevitable moments of darkness and despair.

Over the centuries the Rabbis have evolved a pattern of practices and rites which are concerned with every aspect of death, and these include tender regard for the dying and deep concern for the sorrowing family. The ritual of burial and the manner of mourning are prescribed to preserve, *inter alia*, the qualities of taste and moderation. Moreover, the Sages endeavoured to reconcile the natural and spontaneous expression of profound grief with the reasoned and resigned self-control that the believing Jew is enjoined to practise. Jewish laws of mourning are many and detailed but they always are inspired with a warm humanity; this is in pursuance of the guiding principles of the Rabbis, always to adopt the 'lenient view' when questions arose in connection with the laws of mourning.

Beginning with the work *Torat Ha-Adam* by Rabbi Moses ben Nachman (1194–1270) and the publication of *Maavar Yabok* by the Italian Cabbalist Berachiah ben Moses of

Modena (d. 1638), a vast Hebrew literature on the subject of mourning has been evolved, culminating with Rabbi Leopold Greenwald's *Kol Bo Al Avelut* (On Laws of Mourning) published between 1947 and 1952. Yet, apart from the translation of Rabbi Simon Frankforter's *Sepher Chayyim* (The Book of Life) by the Rev. Benjamin Henry Ascher (1812–93) published in 1847, 'The Handbook of Life,' issued by the *Chevrah Kadisha* of London in 1909 and 'Eternal Life,' by Rabbi J. S. Sperka, published in 1939, little has been written on the subject in English.

The present book is not designed to be an exhaustive compendium of the laws of mourning, nor is it intended to supplant or supersede the authorised Rabbinic Codes. It is merely intended as an elementary guide for the layman who should in all cases of doubt seek the advice of competent rabbinical authorities who alone have the power to give decisions in the light of individual circumstances.

I desire to express my thanks to all who were helpful to me in preparing the book, particularly to Rabbi Dr M. Ginsberg, Dr Alexander Tobias, the Rev. J. Israelstam and Rabbi Dr S. Goldman for reading the manuscript and making many valuable suggestions. I am grateful to Mr Max Epstein for the keen interest he has taken in this publication.

H.R.

NOTE:—The two most used abbreviations in the book are:—

A.P.B. The Authorised Daily Prayer Book, 2nd revised edition, 1962.

Y.D. *Yoreh Deah* by Rabbi Joseph Caro (1488–1575).

CHAPTER

I

THE WAY OF ALL FLESH

VISITING the Sick—*Bikkur Cholim*—is one of the many social obligations which Judaism has clothed with religious significance. Even God Himself is said to have observed this *Mitzvah*,[1] and man is enjoined to follow this Divine example.

Bikkur Cholim is classified by the *Mishnah*[2] as one of those precepts 'the fruit of which a man enjoys in this world, while the stock remains for him in the world to come.' It is an act which benefits the visitor almost as much as the sick person. When a friend or neighbour is ill, a man should not be indifferent. He should regard it his duty to visit the sufferer regardless of the invalid's age, colour or race.[3]

Thoughtless visits, however, are to be discouraged for they may hinder rather than help the patient's progress. The visitor is, therefore, urged to disregard his personal inclinations and to consider only the patient's welfare. Visiting too early in the morning or too late at night is to be avoided.[4] 'Do not fatigue him by staying too long,' counsels Rabbi Eleazar ben Isaac of Worms, the eleventh century moralist, 'for his malady is heavy enough already.

---

[1] 'The Holy One, Blessed be He, visited the sick, for it is written: "And the Lord appeared unto him by the oaks of Mamre" (Gen. XVIII: 1) so do thou also visit the sick' (*Sotah* 14a).

[2] *Mishnah Peah* Ch. I; *Shabbat* 127a.

[3] *Gittin* 61a; Y.D. 335.9 'One must visit the sick of the Gentiles so as to promote good will.'

[4] *Nedarim* 40a; Y.D. 335.4.

Enter cheerfully, for his heart and his eyes are on those who come in.'[1]

Merely to visit a patient is not necessarily the true fulfilment of the *Mitzvah*. *Bikkur Cholim* was never envisaged by our Sages as a mere passive and perfunctory convention.[2] If the sick person is in want, then his needs must be satisfied. 'My son,' advised Rabbi Eleazar, 'when thou visitest a sick man who is without means, be quick to offer refreshments to him and he will esteem it as though thou didst uphold and restore his soul. The Lord will requite thee.'[3] But even when a patient has ample means and is well cared for, the visitor is expected to add to his comfort by giving practical expression of his sympathy. If one cannot visit a sick person by all means enquire even if only by telephone, but the *Mitzvah* of *Bikkur Cholim* cannot be fulfilled by the enquiry; only warm contact can give the patient the reassurance and the comforting knowledge he needs, in the hours of pain and weakness, that he is not left to suffer alone.

Although it is obviously important to minister to the physical needs of the patient and to relieve him of those material worries which might retard healing or even aggravate his illness, nevertheless, the best help is prayer, which is an indispensable part of *Bikkur Cholim*.[4] There are many references in the Bible and Talmud to prayers for the sick.[5]

Selected Psalms may be read, particularly Psalm CXIX, which consists of twenty-two stanzas corresponding to the letters of the Hebrew alphabet. Well-wishers for the good of the patient often fast or visit the graves of loved ones or give charity 'which delivereth from death.'[6] At the Reading of the

---

[1] *Hebrew Ethical Wills*, ed. Israel Abrahams, Vol. I p. 40.
[2] *Berachot* 5b.
[3] Abrahams, *op. cit.*, p. 44.
[4] Y.D. 335.5.
[5] Gen. xx: 17; Num. XII: 13; Isa. XXXVIII: 2–5; *Nedarim* 40a; *Shabbat* 12b; *Berachot* 34b.
[6] Prov. x: 2; XI: 4.

Law a special *Mi-Sheberach* may be recited.[1]

Where the illness is grave more serious measures should be taken. The patient may be given an additional name, such as *Chayyim* (or *Chayah*), *Yechiel*, *Raphael*, *Benzion*, *Alter* (or *Alta*). In the Talmud Rabbi Isaac affirms that the 'changing of a name' is one of the four things which cancel the doom of a man.[2] This custom known as *Shinnui Hashem* (Change of Name) is mentioned by Rabbi Judah ben Samuel Ha-Chassid (d. 1217)[3] and by many mediaeval Rabbinic authorities.[4]

When the name of the sick person is mentioned in a *Mi-Sheberach*, it is customary to refer to the name of the mother and not to that of the father. The *Zohar*[5] traces this custom to David who prayed to God, 'Save the son of Thy handmaid' (Ps. LXXXVI: 16).

Nothing must be allowed to stand in the way of preserving or prolonging life. 'It is a religious precept,' states the Talmud,[6] 'to desecrate the Sabbath for any person afflicted with an illness that may prove dangerous.' The Rabbis give this graphic illustration: 'For a day-old child (who is dangerously ill) the Sabbath may be profaned; however, for the dead, be he even David, the king of Israel, the Sabbath must not be violated.'[7]

Human life is precious and its preservation takes precedence over every other consideration. A sick person should not be given bad news, nor should he be told of the death of a relative lest he be so distressed that his recovery is retarded.[8]

---

[1] J. H. Hertz, *Authorised Daily Prayer Book*, p. 492.
[2] *Rosh Hashanah* 16b.
[3] *Sepher Ha-Chassidim* Nos. 244, 245 (ed Wistinetzki, par. 365).
[4] Isserlein, *Terumat Hadeshen*, No. 234; Weil, *Responsa*, No. 182; cf. H. J. Zimmels, *Magicians, Theologians and Doctors*, p. 143.
[5] J. D. Eisenstein, *Ozar Dinim Uminhagim*, p. 220.
[6] *Yoma* 85a and Code *Orach Chayyim* 328.2.
[7] *Shabbat* 151b.
[8] Y.D. 337.1; *Moed Katan* 26b.

Sabbath is a good day for visiting the sick.[1] In mediaeval times it was customary in many communities for the worshippers to pay such visits before returning home to eat the Sabbath meal. In 1360 Rabbi Nissim ben Reuben Gerondi, the foremost Halachic authority of his time, refers to a Society for Visiting the Sick.

PHYSICIANS

God Himself is the supreme physician 'who healeth the broken in heart, and bindeth up their wounds' (Ps. CXLVII: 3). Three times a day, Jews pray for heaven-sent healing: 'Heal us, O Lord, and we shall be healed; save us and we shall be saved; for Thou art our praise. Grant a perfect healing to all our wounds; for Thou, almighty King, art a faithful and merciful physician. Blessed art thou, O Lord, who healest the sick of Thy people Israel.'[2]

Nevertheless, the Rabbis readily conceded that the Divine Healer does His work through mortals and thus physicians were held in high regard.[3] Joseph employed house physicians (Gen. L: 2), and a physician was in attendance in the Courts of Law.[4] This was not in any way a usurpation of Divine prerogative, since the Torah itself, the Rabbis assure us, granted the physician authority to heal.[5] 'Honour a physician,' advises Ben Sira, 'according to thy need of him, with the honours due unto him; for verily the Lord hath created him.' (Eccl. xxxviii: 1-2.)

In mediaeval times many of our great Rabbis were physicians. The celebrated bibliographer, Moritz Steinschneider (1816-1907) listed 2,168 Jewish physicians

[1] *Orach Chayyim* 287.1.

[2] A.P.B. p. 49.

[3] *Baba Meziah* 85b; *Chullin* 7b; *Sanhedrin* 17b; *Bet Yoseph* Y.D.336.

[4] *Makkot* 22b.

[5] *Baba Kamma* 85a. The school of R. Ishmael taught: 'And the words "And he shall cause him to be thoroughly healed" (Ex. xxi: 19) are the source whence it can be derived that authority was granted by God to the medical man to heal,' *Berachot* 60a.

who are known to have lived between the Dark Ages and the eighteenth century.[1]

It is the doctor's duty to prolong life as long as possible and he must not allow any consideration to weaken the patient's power of resistance. 'Even when the physician realises that his patient approaches death, he should order him to eat this and not to eat that, drink this and not to drink that, but on no account should he tell him that the end is near.'[2]

MERCY KILLING

Euthanasia (painless killing) for sufferers from incurable diseases is contrary to the teachings of Judaism. The account given of the burning at the stake of Rabbi Chaninah ben Tradyon (a *Tanna* of the second century) states that his disciples were anxious to save him unnecessary pain. 'Open thy mouth', they pleaded, 'so that the fire enter into thee. 'He replied: 'Let Him who gave my soul take it away, but no one should injure oneself.'[3] However, he permitted the executioner to remove from over his heart the tufts of wool which had been put there to increase his torture by delaying his death.

Our Sages believed that a 'man who destroys a single soul is regarded as having destroyed an entire world.'[4] Hence no direct action to hasten death is permitted.

VIDDUY—CONFESSION

A patient nearing his end should be encouraged to confess his sins before God, for such a time calls for sincere penitence and evokes God's forgiveness. No confessor is needed since only God can absolve sin. The patient is urged: 'Confess your sins! Many confessed their sins and died not, and many who have not confessed died; and as a

---

[1] Cecil Roth, *The Jewish Contribution to Civilisation*, p. 192.
[2] Ecclesiastes *Rabbah* v.6.
[3] *Avodah Zarah* 18a.
[4] *Sanhedrin* 37a.

reward, should you confess, you will live; and he who confesses his sins has a portion in the world to come.'[1]

The following is a brief form of confession: 'I acknowledge unto thee, O Lord my God and God of my fathers, that both my cure and my death are in Thy hands. May it be Thy will to send me to a perfect healing. Yet if my death be fully determined by Thee, I will in love accept it at Thy hand. O may my death be an atonement for all my sins, iniquities and transgressions of which I have been guilty against Thee. Bestow upon me the abounding happiness that is treasured up for the righteous. Make known to me the path of life: in Thy presence is fulness of joy; at Thy right hand, bliss for evermore.

Thou who art the father of the fatherless and judge of the widow, protect my beloved kindred with whose soul my own is knit. Into Thy hand I commend my spirit; Thou hast redeemed me, O Lord of Truth. Amen, and Amen.'[2]

If one does not know that confession should be said, others should tell him to say 'May my death be an atonement.' However, such things should not be said to him in the presence of women and children for it may make them weep and cause the sick person distress.[3] This rite may be performed on the Sabbath and on Holy Days.

LAST WILL AND TESTAMENT

Our Sages relate that when Jacob felt that his end was near he asked for Divine mercy: 'Lord of the world!' he prayed, 'May it please Thee to grant that a man should fall ill for two or three days and then be gathered into his people, in order that he may have time to put his house in order and repent of his sins.' The Holy One replied: 'It shall be so and thou shalt be the first to profit by the new dispen-

[1] Y.D. 338.1.
[2] A.P.B., pp. 419–420; Y.D. 338.
[3] *Ibid.*, Y.D. 338.1.

THE WAY OF ALL FLESH

sation,'[1] and so it happened that Jacob fell sick a little while before his death.

Thus the blessing of Jacob,[2] the final requests of Joseph,[3] the farewell address of Moses,[4] the advice of David[5] and the last exhortations of Mattathias[6] have set a pattern which runs like a golden thread through Jewish literature. These are remarkable writings, these deathbed declarations of faith which are filled with love of God and humanity, with worldly wisdom and other-worldly visions. 'The testaments,' writes Israel Abrahams,[7] 'give an intimate insight into the personal religion of Jews in various ages. The wills convey much information as to social life, the position of women, habits of dress and domestic economy, schemes of education and, indeed, as to the many interests of business and culture.'

Isaiah's advice to king Hezekiah: 'Set thy house in order, for thou shalt die, and not live' (Isa. xxxviii: 1)[8] has always been taken literally by pious Jews. The Rabbis regarded such final instructions as of paramount importance and they considered the oral testament of a dying person as legally binding as if his instructions had been written down and witnessed.[9]

LAST MOMENTS

A dying man is known as a *Gosess*.[10] Despite the Talmudic

[1] Zohar, *Terumah* 174b; cf. Louis Ginzberg, *The Legends of the Jews*, Vol. II p. 131.
[2] Gen. xlix: 2–27.
[3] Gen. l: 24–25.
[4] Deut. xxxiii: 2–29.
[5] I Kings ii: 1–9.
[6] I Maccabees iii: 49–69.
[7] Abrahams, *op. cit.* xxiv.
[8] Also II Kings xx: 1.
[9] *Gittin* 13a.
[10] Cf. *Targum* on Isa. lx: 4 and *Rema* (*Even Haezer* 121.7 and *Choshen Mishpat* 211.2): 'Brings up a secretion in his throat on account of the narrowing of his chest.'

dictum 'Most *gosessim* die'[1] the Sabbath may be profaned
to prolong their lives even if it is unlikely that they can
survive much longer. Not until life has actually departed
may the services which are normally performed for a dead
person be performed for a *Gosess*.[2]

Those visiting a dying man should not discuss worldly
matters nor eat or drink in his presence.

A dying person should not be left alone. It is a great
Mitzvah to be present at *Yetziat Neshamah* (Departure of the
Soul).[3] When the end is approaching the last paragraph of
the Confession should be recited, especially 'Hear O Israel;
The Lord our God, the Lord is one.'[4]

Death is presumed to occur when breathing appears to
have stopped. The body must then be left untouched for
about eight minutes when a feather is laid across the lips
and nose while those present watch carefully for the
slightest sign of movement. When death is finally established, the eyes and mouth are gently closed by the son or
the nearest relative.

Jacob was assured that Joseph would render this final
filial service (Gen. XLVI: 4).[5] Legend has it that the dying
are granted a glimpse of the Divine. 'Thou canst not see
My face, for men shall not see Me and live' (Ex. XXXIII: 20);
in other words, a man cannot see God in life but only in
death.[6]

When life has departed and the eyes are closed, the arms
and hands are extended at the sides of the body and the

[1] *Gittin* 28a.
[2] Y.D. 339.1.
[3] *Ibid.*, s. 4.
[4] A.P.B., p. 420.
[5] Cf. Commentaries of Ibn Ezra and *Baal Haturim* on Gen.
XLVI: 4.
[6] *Zohar, Vayyechi* 218b: 'At a time of a man's death he is vouch-
safed to see his dead relatives and companions from the other
world.' Also p. 226: 'It is not meet that the eyes which have just
beheld a holy vision should now dwell on a sight of different
character.'

lower jaw is bound up before *rigor mortis* sets in. The body is then placed on the floor with the feet towards the door, and is finally covered with a sheet, while a lighted candle is placed close to the head.

On the Sabbath[1] or on *Yom Tov*[2] the body must not be moved although the chin may be lightly bound. If a Jew dies in a hospital or nursing home, and no fellow Jews are available to perform these services, they may be carried out by the Gentile staff.[3]

The departure of life is sad but never sinister. When Rabbi Simcha Bunam of Psyzcha (1765–1827) was lying on his death bed, his wife wept bitterly, whereupon he said: 'Why dost thou weep? All my life has been given me merely that I might learn how to die.' Death should be regarded simply as a transition, a move from one home to another, from the lower world into the higher. A believing Jew echoes the words of the Psalmist, 'Yea, though I walk through the valley of the shadow of death, I will fear no evil, for Thou art with me' (Ps. XXIII: 4).

[1] *Orach Chayyim*, 311.1.
[2] *Ibid.*, 526.3 and *Mishnah Berurah, ad loc.*
[3] A circular entitled 'Guidance for Hospital Authorities' issued by the office of the Sexton, Burial Society of the United Synagogue (January, 1960) reads as follows: 'Where it is not possible to obtain the services of a Jewish chaplain, it is permissible for the hospital staff to carry out the following: Close the eyes. Tie up the jaw. Keep arms and hands straight, by sides of the body. Any tubes or instruments in the body should be removed and the incision plugged. The corpse should then be wrapped in a plain sheet without religious emblems, and placed in the mortuary or other special room for Jewish bodies.'

CHAPTER

II

RESPECT FOR THE DEAD

THE body, the creation of God and the dwelling place of the soul, must be accorded every respect. *Kevod Hamet*, respect for the dead, is a fundamental principle of Judaism. The first mention of this concept is in the Bible: 'And Hezekiah slept with his fathers . . . and the inhabitants of Jerusalem did him honour at his death' (II Chron. XXXII: 33).

Judaism, always more concerned with deeds than with words, defines our duties to the living and details our obligation to the dead. The Biblical heroes were demonstrative in their expressions of grief. Abraham, we are told, 'came to mourn for Sarah, and to weep for her' (Gen. XXIII: 2), and Jacob 'mourned for his son (Joseph) many days' (Gen. XXXVII: 34), while Joseph 'fell upon his father's face, and wept upon him, and kissed him' (Gen. L: 1). Then there is David's moving reaction to the death of Saul as we read: 'And they wailed, and wept, and fasted until even, for Saul, and for Jonathan his son, and for the people of the Lord, and for the house of Israel; because they were fallen by the sword' (II Sam. 1: 12).

The Rabbis, though they were opposed to excessive display of grief, stressed that the dead should be mourned in a fitting manner. 'If one sheds tears for a worthy person, the Holy One, Blessed be He, counts them and lays them up in His treasure house . . . Whoever weeps for a worthy man is forgiven all his iniquities on account of the honour which he showed him.'[1] Consideration for the dead is an act of

[1] *Shabbat* 105b.

lovingkindness devoid of the self-interest which sometimes mars human relationships.

Our Rabbis forbade men to slander or speak in derogatory terms of the dead. The Midrash quotes God as reproving Moses for making disparaging reference to the ancestors of his generation. Among the twenty-four offences punishable by excommunication, which in the Talmudic and Middle Ages meant social ostracism and economic ruin, was 'insulting a learned man even after death.'[1]

After mentioning the name of a dead person it is customary to add the phrase *Alav Hashalom* 'May peace be to him' or *Zichrono Livrachah* 'May his memory be for a blessing.' If the deceased was a pious man one should say *Zecher Zaddik Livrachah* 'May the memory of the righteous be for a blessing.'

In the first year of mourning, the formula is *Hareni Kaparat Mishkavo*[2] 'May I be his (or her) atonement.'

WATCHERS (*WACHERS*)

A dead body should not be left alone. It must be guarded night and day on weekdays as well as on Sabbath until the funeral. Such was the importance attached by the Rabbis to this rite, that the watchers did not have to say prayers or put on *Tephillin* while attending to their duties.[3] The reasons which have been given are varied. Some have suggested that it was to keep away evil spirits, others to protect the body from rodents and body snatchers; but the most probable explanation is that it is a mark of respect for the dead since it is considered disrespectful to leave a human body in a defenceless state unattended.

It is forbidden to have a meal in the room where a dead person is lying. Only matters concerned with the deceased may be pursued in the presence of the corpse.

The watchers should spend the time reciting verses from

[1] *Berachot* 19a.
[2] *Kiddushin* 31b.
[3] Y.D. 341.6.

the Book of Psalms 'which contains the whole music of the heart swept by the hand of his Maker. In it are gathered the lyrical burst of his tenderness, the moan of his penitence, the pathos of his sorrow, the triumph of his victory, the despair of his defeat, the firmness of his confidence, the rapture of his assured hope. In it is presented the anatomy of all parts of the human soul; in it, as Heine says, "are collected sunrise and sunset, birth and death, promise and fulfilment—the whole drama of humanity" . . . To weary travellers of every condition and at every period of history, the Psalms, then, are a mirror in which each man sees the motions of his own soul. They express in exquisite words the kinship which every thoughtful human heart craves to find with a supreme, unchanging, loving God, who will be to him a protector, guardian and a friend . . . They translate into speech the spiritual passion of the loftiest genius; they also utter, with beauty born of truth and simplicity, and with the exact agreement between the feelings and the expressions, the inarticulate and humble longings of the unlettered peasant . . . They alone have known no limitations to a particular age, country or form of faith. In the Psalms the vast hosts of suffering humanity have found the deepest expressions of their hopes and fears.'[1]

EARLY BURIAL

It is obligatory upon Jews to bury the dead as soon as possible, and early burial has always been the Jewish practice.[2] In 1772 when the Duke of Mecklenburg-Schwerin prohibited burial before the lapse of three days the leading Rabbinical authorities protested vigorously.

---

[1] R. E. Prothero, *The Psalms in Human Life*, pp. 1–5.
[2] Cf. Deut. XXI: 23 'His body shall not remain all night upon the tree but thou shalt surely bury him the same day.' The *Mishnah Sanhedrin* 46b states: 'Whoever leaves his dead lie over night, transgresses both a positive command ("but thou shalt surely bury him the same day") and the negative command "his body shall not remain all night upon the tree." '

Early burial was not due entirely to the exigencies of the hot climate of the Holy Land, as it is sometimes said. Rather it was considered a humiliation to the dead to leave them unburied.

However, a delay in burial is permitted if it is 'for the sake of his honour', e.g., for the purpose of making a coffin or providing shrouds, or to enable relatives and friends to pay their last respects.[1]

In Britain no arrangements for a funeral may be made 'until the Sexton has received the requisite (interment) certificate, issued by the Registrar (of Births and Deaths) under the Birth and Deaths (Registration) Act 1926, and if an inquest shall have been ordered, the Coroner's Order for Burial.'[2]

POST MORTEM EXAMINATION

It is forbidden to carry out an autopsy to ascertain the cause of death unless the civil authorities so order. For the same reason dissection is regarded as dishonouring the human body, an insult to the dead and an infringement of the principle which forbids any benefit to be derived from the dead. This prohibition was upheld by Rabbi Ezekiel ben Judah Landau[3] (1713–1793) and Rabbi Moses Schreiber (1763–1839).[4]

Today in the state of Israel, the Chief Rabbinate sanctions a post mortem examination when (a) it is legally required; (b) in the opinion of three doctors, the cause of death cannot otherwise be ascertained; (c) it might help to save the lives of others suffering from maladies similar to that from which the patient died; and (d) in cases of certain hereditary diseases, so as to safeguard surviving relatives.[5]

---

[1] *Sanhedrin* 47a; Y.D. 357.1.

[2] *Laws and Bye-laws of the Burial Society*, F. 2, p. 59.

[3] *Noda Beyehudah*, part II, Y.D., No. 210.

[4] *Chatam Sopher* Y.D. No. 336.

[5] M. D. Silberstein, 'Baayat Nituah Hametim Upitrona' in *Yavneh*, 1949, p. 214 ff., quoted by Immanuel Jakobovits, *Jewish Medical Ethics*, New York, 1959, p. 150.

Moreover 'The Plenary Council of the Chief Rabbinate of Israel . . . do not object to the use of bodies of persons who gave their consent in writing of their own free will during their lifetime for anatomical dissections as required for medical studies, provided the dissected parts are carefully preserved so as to be eventually buried with due respect according to Jewish Law.'[1]

It is interesting to note that a former British Chief Rabbi Hermann Adler, in the memorial address which he delivered on January 24, 1905, on the death of the philanthropist Frederic David Mocatta (1828–1905) stated: 'His selflessness is proved by a remarkable instruction he gave to his physician. He directed that, in the event of his dying of an obscure disease, after death examination should be made, the cost being borne by his estate, for the advancement of medical science and for the benefit of those who might suffer hereafter from a similar ailment.'[2]

TRANSPLANTING THE EYES OF THE DECEASED

Although a number of rabbinic authorities forbid the transplanting of the cornea from a dead person on account of the inevitable mutilation, most rabbinic scholars permit it under certain safeguards on the ground that it will help to restore sight to the living.[3] Where a person expressly bequeaths his eyes for the benefit of another, irrespective of the consequent mutilation to his own body, such instructions may be obeyed. Laws which may appear stringent are interpreted leniently when life is at stake.

With regard to the hair of the dead, the consensus of opinion is to permit its use for the living.[4]

---

[1] *Dat Yisrael Umedinat Yisrael*, 1951, p. 161; Eliezer Judah Waldenburg, *Tzitz Eliezer*, Jerusalem, 1954, part IV, no. 14, quoted by Jakobovits, *op. cit.*, p. 150.

[2] Adler, *Anglo-Jewish Memories*, London, 1909, p. 137.

[3] Dayan M. Steinberg, *Responsum*, London, 1957, p. 12.

[4] Y.D. 349.2 cf. *Keseph Mishnah* to *Yad Evel*, Greenwald, *op. cit.*, p. 57.

EMBALMING

Embalming was specifically an Egyptian rite and the Bible records only two cases, those of Jacob and Joseph (Gen. L: 2 and 26). In later times we read that the body of Aristobulus II, king of Judea (67–63 B.C.E.)[1] was also embalmed. This practice, however, was contrary to Jewish usage.[2]

If transportation to another city or country should be necessary, ecclesiastical authorities should be consulted. During the summer months, an ice-box may be used before the *Taharah*, if necessary.[3]

CREMATION

Traditional Judaism is unequivocally opposed to cremation for a number of reasons. Firstly, it is, like embalming, contrary to Jewish usage, since from earliest recorded times, Jews have invariably buried their dead in the earth, for it is written 'dust thou art and to dust thou shalt return' (Gen. III: 19). Our Sages[4] trace the rite of burial to the beginning of mankind and relate that Adam and Eve were greatly distressed when they saw the dead body of Abel, their son, and they did not know how to dispose of it. Then a raven took pity on them. The grief-stricken parents observed how it scratched the earth away in one spot and then hid a dead bird of its own kind in the ground. In like manner Adam dealt with his son.[4] Henceforth the heroes of the Bible from Abraham to the kings of Israel were interred in the ground.

Additional evidence that burial was the traditional Jewish method is provided by the Roman historian Tacitus

[1] Josephus, *Antiquities* XVI: 7.
[2] 'Why did Joseph die before his brethren?' Rabbi said: 'Because he embalmed his father.' Genesis *Rabbah* 100.2.
[3] Moses Hyamson, *Rules and Regulations of the Chevra Kadisha Orach Chaim*, N.Y., 1942, p. 7.
[4] *Pirke de Rabbi Eliezer* Ch. XXI (ed. G. Friedlander, London, 1916), p. 156; *Tanchumah* (Vilna, 1833). Genesis x and Genesis *Rabbah* XXII: 8 reads 'Two clean birds.'

(55–120 B.C.E.) who writes: 'They [the Jews] bury rather than burn their dead.'[1]

'Burning' was one of the 'four deaths' imposed by the Biblical penal code for a number of offences.[2] 'Bring her forth and let her be burnt' (Gen. XXXVIII: 24), Judah said when told of Tamar's unchastity. 'Achan and his family were stoned and their bodies were burnt' (Josh. VII: 25). These are but two examples of this penalty being carried out. Yet so abhorrent was burning to the Rabbis that, unlike the Sadducees, they did not take it literally.[3] The act of reducing the human body to ashes was to them unthinkable.

Our Sages teach that cremation is an indignity, an affront to man as the highest form of creation. The body, the temple and the servant of the soul must be guarded against sacrilegious desecration.

In Rabbinic writings burning was described as an idolatrous practice. 'Every death which is accompanied by burning,' say the Rabbis, 'is looked upon as idolatry.'[4] The record of the idolatrous kings who caused their children to pass 'through the fire to Molech in the valley of the Children of Hinnom'[5] associated burning with paganism. Legend has it that in order to avoid divine judgment, Titus, who destroyed the second Temple in the year 70 C.E., instructed his descendants to burn his body and scatter the ashes over the seven seas 'so that the God of the Jews should not find me and bring me to trial.'[6] The Roman practice of cremation and their worship of ancestral ashes as household

[1] Hist. V. 5.

[2] Lev. XXI: 9; XVIII: 10; XX: 14; *Sanhedrin*, IX: 1; *Sifra, Kedoshim*, IX. 16; *Yevamot* 21a.

[3] 'Molten lead or a mixture of lead and tin' was poured down the throat of the criminal. *Sanhedrin* VII.2; *Yerushalmi, Sanhedrin* VII.24b.

[4] *Avodah Zarah* I.3. Both Rashi and Bertinoro explain the *Mishnah* 'Death at which burning of articles of the dead takes place is attended by idolatry.'

[5] II Kings XXIII: 10; II Chron. XXIII: 3 and XXVIII: 3.

[6] *Gittin* 56b.

gods were additional reasons for classifying cremation as *Chukat hagoy* (pagan custom).

Maimonides considers burial a Scriptural injunction and rules that if one leaves a testamentary injunction not to be buried, his wishes are ignored in this matter.[1]

Nevertheless there are a number of references in the Bible sufficiently interesting and unusual to merit careful study. In the first Book of Samuel (xxxi: 12) we read that 'when the inhabitants of Jabesh Gilead heard concerning him that which the Philistines had done to Saul, all the valiant men arose, and went all night and took the body of Saul and the bodies of his sons from the wall of Beth-Shan; and they came to Jabesh, and burnt them there.' This was surely an extraordinary incident, a desperate action designed to save the corpses from further indignity at the enemy's hands. Yet even in this instance the parallel passage in the Book of Chronicles merely states that 'their bones were buried' (I Chron. x: 12).[2]

The passage applied to king Asa, 'And they buried him in his own sepulchres which he had hewn out for himself in the city of David, and laid him in the bed which was filled with sweet odours and divers kinds (of spices) prepared by the perfumers' art; and they made a very great burning for him' (II Chron. xvi: 14) clearly refers to the burning not of the body but of spices and plants.

Evidence that such was the practice may be found in the Talmudic passage which states that when Patriarch Gamaliel II (c. 80–110 C.E.) died, Onkelos, commonly called the Proselyte Onkelos,[3] author of the best known Aramaic translation of the Pentateuch (*Targum*) 'burned in his honour articles worth seventy

[1] *Hilchot Avel* xii.1; *Sepher Hamitzvot* No. 231; Y.D. 362.1.

[2] Also Josephus states: 'And they buried the bodies in their fairest country called Aroura,' *Jewish Antiquities* vi:375 (ed. H. St. J. Thackeray, p. 357).

[3] He is often confused with the other proselyte Aquila; *v.* Kohut *Aruch* Vol. I, p. 158.

Tyrian *maneh*.'[1] It was evidently the practice to honour the dead by burning spices and other materials.

RESURRECTION AND CREMATION

Belief in resurrection is a principle of Judaism, as can be seen from our liturgy. When Maimonides said 'There are no material bodies in the future world'[2] he was referring to life after death. But he himself believed that there would be a resurrection for the righteous in this world, and this tradition of a physical[3] as well as a spiritual resurrection has persisted and has been accepted throughout the ages.

Ezekiel's vision of the dry bones (Chapter XXXVII) is taken by our Sages to imply that the 'righteous are destined to arise (from the dead) clothed in all their garments.'[4] This physical resurrection, our Sages tell us,[5] will begin from a bone called *Luz*, the nut spinal column (*Os Coccyx*).

Cremation is thus a denial of the belief in bodily resurrection.

BURIAL OF THE ASHES

In November 1887, the British Chief Rabbi, Nathan Marcus Adler (1803–1890), wrote to Nathaniel Mayer, the first Lord Rothschild (1840–1915), President of the United Synagogues of London: 'With reference to the religious bearings on the question, I beg to state that whilst there does not exist any precept prohibiting the interment in a Jewish cemetery of the ashes of a person who has already been cremated, our law is decidedly and emphatically opposed to the practice of cremation. Both Jewish law and usage require the interment of the bodies of the dead and view the reduction of a corpse to ashes by fire as an indignity

[1] The *maneh* was a weight in gold or silver equal to fifty holy or a hundred common *shekels*. One *maneh* of Tyrian weight equals 25 *selas*.

[2] Essay on Resurrection.

[3] Saadia, *Emunot Vedeot* VII.8.

[4] *Sanhedrin* 90b.

[5] Leviticus *Rabbah* XVIII; Genesis *Rabbah* XXVIII.3.

and an outrage. This can be proved by several passages in the Holy Scriptures, e.g. Amos II: 1 where punishment is denounced upon Moab 'because he burned the bones of the King of Edom into lime." '[1]

Four years later (27 September, 1891) the wife of Dr Maurice Davis was cremated and Chief Rabbi Dr Hermann Adler, the son of Nathan Marcus Adler, was asked for a ruling on the interment of the ashes. 'I have given this request my full consideration in concert with the members of the *Beth Din*,' he wrote in reply. 'We subscribe to the opinion stated by my venerated Predecessor, that there does not exist any precept prohibiting the interment in a Jewish cemetery of the ashes of a person who has already been cremated, an opinion supported by other eminent Rabbis including the Chief Rabbi of Kovno [Rabbi Isaac Elchanan Spector, 1817–1896]. We accordingly permit such a burial. At the same time we earnestly beg you and the members of the community not to construe this permission into a sanction of the practice of cremation. We ardently hope that no brother or sister in faith will make a similar testamentary disposition, involving, as it does, a grave breach of Jewish law.'[2]

A bye-law of the Burial Society of the United Synagogue of London states: 'The society shall not make any arrangements whatever for cremation. Where cremation is nevertheless to take place a Service may be held at the house prior to the removal of the body, and if the ashes be encoffined then interment may take place at a Cemetery of the United Synagogue and the Burial Service shall be conducted there at the time of the interment.'[3]

On the other hand, the other London Orthodox Synagogal bodies, the Federation of Synagogues and the Union of Orthodox Hebrew Congregations do not permit the ashes of cremated persons to be buried in their cemeteries.

[1] *The Jewish Chronicle*, December 9, 1887 and September 3, 1926.
[2] *The Jewish Chronicle*, October 2, 1891, p. 10.
[3] F. 14, p. 61.

CHAPTER

III

THE PERIOD OF ANINUT

UNTIL the burial of the deceased the mourner is known as an *Onen*.[1] The interval between death and burial is called *Aninut*. After the interment these two terms are superseded by the words *Avel* and *Avelut* respectively.

While having to abide by the negative precepts of the Torah, the *Onen* is absolved from the performance of all the religious duties enjoined in the Torah[2] such as the recital of prayers or the putting on of *Tephillin*. There are two reasons for this: firstly to enable him to attend without distraction to the needs of the dead, since nothing must interfere with the preparations for burial, and 'he who is engaged in a religious act is exempt from performing other religious duties'[3]: secondly, there must be no lessening of the honour and respect accorded to the deceased.[4]

Although today in most communities there are well organised burial societies which efficiently carry out all the detailed duties, the *Onenim* still have the responsibility of approaching and making arrangements with the burial society as well as obtaining death and other certificates which may be required before the funeral can take place. They must also inform relatives and friends so as to

[1] Lit. 'Trouble or sorrow' cf. Gen. xxxv: 18 *Ben Oni* 'Son of my trouble' and Hosea (ix: 4) 'bread of mourning.'

[2] *Moed Katan* 23b: Y.D. 341.1.

[3] *Sukkah* 25a.

[4] *Semachot* x.

ensure that all honour and respect is paid to the deceased.[1]

The *Onen*, as has been mentioned, does not recite prayers or put on *Tephillin*.[2] But he is forbidden to eat meat or drink wine[3] or over-indulge in eating.[4] When he eats bread, he must wash his hands but is not required to recite the benediction thereof. He must not be gainfully occupied. Only in cases where great hardship might be incurred may he complete his unfinished tasks, provided they do not interfere with or in any way delay the funeral arrangements. A minor is not subject to the laws of *Aninut*.

If death occurs on the Sabbath, or if the Sabbath is part of the *Aninut* period, the *Onen* must perform the same *Mitzvot* as anyone else.[5] He may also eat meat and drink wine on that day.[6] However, he is not to study the Torah or be called up to the Reading of the Law in the Synagogue.[7] The same rulings apply to Festivals.

A *Cohen* who is an *Onen* may not recite the Priestly Blessings (*Duchaning*) during the Additional Service on a Festival. Only if no other *Cohen* is available may he officiate at the Redemption of the first-born (*Pidyon ha-ben*), a ceremony which must take place on the thirty-first day after birth. If the *Onen* officiates, the benediction over the wine is recited by another person. On *Yom Kippur*, the *Onen* must obey every requirement of the Fast day. However, the duties to the dead take precedence over the *Mitzvah* of building a *Sukkah*[8] and the *Onen* is not required to *Bensch*

---

[1] Some authorities maintain that 'in a place where there is a *Chevrah Kadisha* the relatives are not legally subject to the laws of *Aninut* and are obliged to read the *Shema* and recite the *Amidah*.' *Kitzur Shulchan Aruch* 196.5.

[2] *Mishnah Berachot* III: 1.

[3] *Berachot* 17b.

[4] *Yerushalmi Berachot* III: 1.

[5] *Moed Katan* 23b; Y.D. 341.1.

[6] *Ibid* and *Berachot* 18a.

[7] Greenwald, *Kol Bo Al Avelut*, p. 130.

[8] If, however, he is not preoccupied with the burial arrangements he is obliged to build a *Sukkah*.

31

etrog (pronounce the blessing over the Four Species on *Chol Hamoed*).

On Passover he must eat *Matzah* and drink the Four Cups of wine during the *Seder* service. However, he is not required to recite the *Haggadah*[1] nor to count the *Omer*.[2] He should delegate to another person the ceremony of the Search for the Leaven on the eve of the fourteenth day of *Nisan*. He may, however, recite the declaration *Kol Chamira*[3] (all manner of leaven). On *Chanukah*, he should not kindle the lights if it is possible to delegate this to another member of the household. On *Purim* he may go to the Synagogue to hear the *Megillah* (Book of Esther)[4] and it is permitted to eat meat and drink wine during the day.[5] Yet on the 9th of *Av* he may not go to the Synagogue to hear the Book of Lamentations and *Kinot* (Elegies and Lamentations).[6]

If the only Rabbi in the town becomes an *Onen* he may decide ritual questions.[7] But a Reader who is an *Onen* may not officiate in the Synagogue.[8] An *Onen* who is a *Shochet* (a ritual slaughterer) may slaughter during the period of *Aninut*[9] and a beadle may attend to his duties on the Sabbath and on Festivals. An *Onen* who is a *Mohel* may circumcise his own and other children if there is no other *Mohel* available. The *Brit Milah* (Covenant of circumcision) may take place before the burial and the Benedictions can be recited by others. A circumcision generally takes

[1] He may do so if there is no one else.

[2] He may recite it on the following day without a benediction, *Mishnah Berurah Biur Halachah*, 489.

[3] Chayyim Joseph David Azulai, *Birke Yoseph*.

[4] *Mishnah Berurah*, 696: 13.

[5] But not at night because at night he is not obliged to feast. *Kitzur Shulchan Aruch* 142: 21.

[6] Greenwald, *op. cit.*, p. 137, in the name of Elijah ben Wolf Spiro in *Elijahu Rabbah* (Sulzbach, 1757), p. 157*b*.

[7] Greenwald, *op. cit.* p. 151.

[8] If there is no other person he may officiate: *Kitzur Shulchan Aruch* 196.9.

[9] Some authorities forbid it, cf. *Joseph Daat*.

precedence over the interment of the dead.[1]

If a person receives news of the death of a relative in another city, he becomes subject to the laws of *Aninut* if there are no other relatives residing in the town where the deceased lived. However, if he is notified that the burial will take place on a certain day and distance makes it impossible for him to attend, then he is not subject to the laws of *Aninut*.

Even if a man leaves directions that only one of his children should occupy himself with the burial arrangements, nevertheless, the status of *Aninut* falls on all the children. If the *Onen* is already a mourner for his father or his mother or if he has *Yahrzeit*, he may recite *Kaddish*.[2]

Aninut does not apply in cases of an infant dying within thirty days of birth.[3]

POURING AWAY WATER

'It is a custom', states the Code *Yoreh Deah*[4], 'to pour out all drawn water[5] in the neighbourhood[6] of the corpse.' Explanations of this practice range from the crude suggestion that the Angel of Death cleans his knife in water to the metaphorical concept of the pouring out of the soul before God. The custom has also been ascribed to the primitive practice of providing food for the departed spirit, and to the superstitious belief that thus the spirit can be saved from drowning.

But there are more rational interpretations. It is suggested that the practice was a means of announcing a death, since Jews have always been reluctant to be the bearers of

---

[1] This is the view of Rabbi Solomon b. Yehudah Luria. Isserles, however, maintains that the *Brit* should take place after the interment.

[2] Greenwald, *op. cit.* pp. 155–6.

[3] *Yerushalmi, Yevamot* XI.7.

[4] 339.5.

[5] i.e. water contained in vessels.

[6] i.e. the three houses including the one in which the dead lies.

evil tidings. Hence the pouring away of the water also served to remind the neighbours of their duty to the deceased and to the mourners. Again water stands for life and fertility. Compare the passage in the Book of Psalms (xxII: 15) 'I am poured out like water,' meaning that life is drawing to an end. Thus the pouring out of water symbolises the extinction of life. Some scholars claim that this custom goes back to Biblical times and in support of this theory quote: 'And Miriam died there and was buried there. And there was no water for the congregation' (Num. xx: 1–2).

MIRRORS

It is customary to cover mirrors or turn them to the wall in the House of Mourning. Some hold that this is done to prevent the soul of the departed from being reflected in the glass; others that it is done simply to prevent the mourner from seeing his own sad countenance, thus adding to his grief. Another view is that mirrors, so often associated with vanity, are out of place at such a time. The most rational explanation is the rule which forbids prayer in front of a mirror, since the reflection distracts the attention of worshippers[1] and prayers are normally recited in the house of the mourner.

THE RENDING OF GARMENTS

'One who has suffered a bereavement for which mourning has to be observed must rend his garments.'[1] The origin of this practice of *Keriah* (rending) is found in the Divine Command, given expressly to the priests Aaron, Eleazar and Ithamar, after the death of Nadab and Abihu: 'Let not the hair of your heads go loose, neither rend your clothes' (Lev. x: 6).[2] From this explicit prohibition, it is inferred that everyone else must perform *Keriah*.

[1] *Abudarham, Sepher Abudarham*, ed. Wertheimer (Jerusalem, 1959), p. 371, *Beer Hetev* on *Orach Chayyim* 90. 23.
[2] Y.D. 340.1.

From earliest times the rending of garments has been regarded as a sign of grief. When his sons brought him Joseph's blood-stained coat, 'Jacob rent his garments' (Gen. xxxvii: 34). When the goblet was found in Benjamin's sack, his brothers 'rent their clothes' (Gen. xliv: 13). When David heard of the death of Saul, 'he took hold of his clothes, and rent them; and likewise all the men that were with him' (II Sam. 1: 10).

The Talmud lays it down that 'one who is present at the time of the departure of the soul of a Jewish man or woman is in duty bound to rend his garments.'[1] This ritual is not enforced today, since it might have the effect of deterring people from attending a dying person.

Nowadays, Keriah is only compulsory when the loss is that of a father, mother, wife, husband, brother, sister, son or daughter, half-brother or half-sister.

The rending of the garments must be done either in the house before the funeral or at the cemetery before the interment. The mourner should stand when the rite is performed.[2] 'Then Job stood up and rent his mantle' (1:20).

The custom of standing has been homiletically explained by the former Chief Rabbi Dr J. H. Hertz: 'Meet all sorrow standing upright. The future may be dark, veiled from the eye of mortals—but not the manner in which we are to meet the future. To rail at life, to rebel against a destiny, that has cast our lines in unpleasant places, is of little avail. We cannot lay down terms to life. Life must be accepted on its own terms. But hard as life's terms are, life (it has been finely said) never dictates unrighteousness, unholiness, dishonour.'[3]

The regulations governing Keriah are that a small cut should be made in the garment with a knife and the tear extended by hand to at least one hand-breadth. In support

[1] *Moed Katan* 25a; Y.D. 340.5.
[2] *Ibid.*, 340.1.
[3] *A Book of Jewish Thoughts* (London, 1935), p. 297.

of this the Talmud quotes: 'Then David took hold on his clothes, and rent them' (II Sam. 1: 10), since it has been established that the measure of a garment which man can seize in his hand is a hand-breadth.[1]

The following blessing is recited: 'Blessed art Thou, O Lord our king, king of the Universe, the true Judge.' For parents, a child rends his or her garment on the left side (close to the heart) and for other relatives on the right side. The rent should be made from above downwards and not from side to side.

Keriah is forbidden on the Sabbath or on Festivals and many ecclesiastical authorities do not permit rending on *Chol Hamoed*, insisting that the rite be delayed until the Festival is ended.

In the Anglo-Jewish community *Keriah* is usually carried out on *Chol Hamoed* for close relatives.[2]

In the case of relatives, other than a parent, *Keriah* takes place only if the news has come within thirty days of death, but in the case of a parent, *Keriah* is always obligatory.

The tear for relatives other than parents may be loosely stitched together after seven days, and the edges resewn after thirty days. The tear for a parent, however, may only be stitched together after thirty days but must never be thoroughly repaired. It is likewise forbidden to cut out the part that was rent and to mend the torn part with another piece of material.

The rites of *Keriah* do not apply when the deceased is an infant less than thirty days old.[3]

If the mourner forgets to rend the garments at the proper time but remembers or is reminded during the *Shivah* days,

---

[1] *Moed Katan* 22b; *Sukkah* 32b; *Niddah* 26a.

[2] Y.D. 340.21 (*Rema*), 'It is customary to rend garments only for one's father and mother . . . And in a locality where there is no accepted practice one must rend for all.' Greenwald, *op. cit.* pp. 32-2.

[3] Y.D. 340.30.

he must perform the *Keriah* just the same. 'For all other dead,' states the Code, 'if he has occasion to change his garments during the *Shivah*, he does not again rend them; for one's father and mother, if one changes his garments during the *Shivah* period he must perform *Keriah* on the fresh garments.'[1]

In honour of the Sabbath he should change his garments and not wear torn clothes.

If a relative dies and the mourner in his distress omits to perform *Keriah* and then another of his relatives dies, he must perform two separate *Keriot*; the first rent must be a hand-breadth and then at a distance of three finger-breadths, he should make the second rent. One who had simultaneously heard 'of the death of his father and his mother or of the death of two other relatives, should rend his garments once for his double loss.'[2]

A minor, who has reached the age of instruction, becomes subject to the laws of mourning and must perform *Keriah* in the same way that he must perform all other *Mitzvot*. The garment of a child 'should be slightly rent for him to manifest his grief and to mark his mourning.'[3] *Keriah* is thus obligatory for children under thirteen years of age.

CHEVRAH KADISHA

The *Chevrah Kadisha* (The Holy Association) is the organisation which concerns itself with the burial of the dead. It was already known in Talmudic times. Once, when Rabbi Hamnuna, a fourth-century C.E. Babylonian teacher, came to Daru-Mata (North of Nisibis) he heard the sound of the funerary-bugle and seeing some people carrying on with their work, he said: 'Let the people be under the *Shammeta* (ban). Is there not a person dead in the town?' They told him that there was an Association in the

---

[1] Y.D. 340.14.
[2] *Kitzur Shulchan Aruch* 195.11.
[3] *Ibid*, s. 13; Y.D. 340.27.

town. 'If so,' he replied 'you are allowed to work.'[1]

The *Chevrah Kadisha* carry out a sacred task and even scholars and sages did not consider it beneath their dignity to attend to the dead. Rabbi Eliezer Ashkenazi in 1564 at Prague laid the foundations of an efficient burial society which became the model of all similar bodies. Their *vade mecum* was *Maavar Yabok* (Ford of Yabok)[2] of Aaron Berachiah of Modena (Venice 1626).

In 1695–96 a separate burial society was instituted for the *Ashkenazi* community in London.[3] This was the counterpart of the *Levandores* of the *Sephardim*.

During the Middle Ages it became customary for the *Chevrah Kadisha* to devote one day each year to fasting and prayer. At the close of this day which was usually held on the 7th *Adar*[4] (the date of Moses' death) a *Seudah* (festive meal) was organised for them.

In many large communities the members of the *Chevrah Kadisha* are paid officials of the community.

In 1870 there occurred the merger of the three London Synagogues (the Great, the Hambro' and the New) with their respective Burial Societies. The Scheme of the United Synagogue Act of 1870 laid down that 'there shall be a Society which shall be called 'The Burial Society of the United Synagogue.'

Today, as in ancient times, it is essential that the members of the *Chevrah Kadisha* be observant Jews.

THE *TAHARAH* (RITES OF PURIFICATION)

The rite of the ritual washing of a corpse before burial is derived from the Biblical injunction: 'As he came so shall he go' (Eccl. v: 5). When man is born he is washed and

---

[1] *Moed Katan* 27*b*.

[2] A book containing dissertations, prayers to be offered for the sick and the dead.

[3] Cecil Roth, *History of the Great Synagogue*, p. 17.

[4] Other Associations held the *Seudah* on 33rd of the *Omer* days (18th of *Iyyar*), eve of the new moon of *Shevat* or 15th of *Kislev*.

when he dies he is washed.[1] The *Mishnah* mentions the practice of washing the body.[2]

A separate building, the *Bet Taharah*, in the cemetery, was used for this purpose but nowadays the rite is usually carried out in the home. A candle is kept burning during the ceremony. Among the *Sephardim* it was customary to blow the Shophar during the *Taharah* or the funeral.[3]

The utmost respect must be shown to the body during the *Taharah* and at least two persons should be employed in moving or changing the position of the body. No person assisting at a *Taharah* shall smoke 'while so engaged.'[4]

The purification rite is as follows: the body is laid on the *Taharah* board in the sheet in which it lies. Warm water (about three gallons) must then be poured down the body from the head to the feet. The mouth is covered so that no water should trickle down it. The body is then turned slightly, first on the right side and then on the left, the warm water being poured down on each side as before. The sheet is used to dry each side so that the hands do not touch the body. The nails of the hands and feet are then cleansed. The hair, too, is washed and combed. A further three gallons must be poured over the head so that it should run down over the entire body. The body is then wrapped in clean sheets and properly dried.[5]

Where death is due to infectious or contagious diseases the *Taharah* must be dispensed with. If a woman dies in confinement no *Taharah* is carried out. Similarly, if 'they find a slain Israelite they must bury him in the same condition as they find him.'[6]

---

[1] *Sepher Ha-Chassidim*, 650.
[2] *Shabbat* XXIII.5.
[3] Zimmels, *Ashkenazim and Sephardim*, p. 183.
[4] *Laws and Bye-laws of the Burial Society*, p. 96.
[5] *The Handbook of life*, issued by the *Chevrah Kadisha of* London, pp. 32–3.
[6] Y.D. 364.4.

TACHRICHIM (SHROUDS)

The garments in which the dead are clothed are known as *Tachrichim*[1] from the Hebrew root which means 'to wrap up.' The shrouds should be made from fine white linen. Neither a hem nor a knot of any sort should be made in the shrouds. No corpse must be shrouded in less than three garments. Some pious people even prepare their shrouds during their lifetime, basing the practice on the verse from Amos: 'Prepare to meet thy God, O Israel' (IV: 12).

After the *Taharah*, the *Halbashah* (dressing) commences. The cap or mitre is placed on the head. The breeches are put on, then the shirt and neckcloth, then the surplice and girdle. It is a custom dating from Talmudic times to bury a dead man in the *Tallit* (prayer shawl) which he used during his lifetime after the fringes have been deliberately rendered ritually unfit. The *Tallit* is then spread out in the coffin and the body is carefully transferred there with the face upwards, the legs extended and the arms at the side.[2]

A man distinguished for his piety may also be clad in his *Kittel*.[3] Earth from the Holy Land is often placed in the coffin.

Of the many references in the Talmud to shrouds one states: 'Formerly the expenses of taking the dead out to his burial fell harder on his near-of-kin than his death so that the dead man's near-of-kin abandoned him and fled, until the time of Rabban Gamaliel,[4] who disregarding his own dignity left instructions that he should come out to his burial in flaxen vestments and thereafter the people followed.'[5] Rabbi Papa who lived in the fourth century declared that the dead were buried in a garb worth only one *zuz* (a small Palestinian coin).[6]

[1] *Mishnah Sanhedrin* VI.5.
[2] *The Handbook of life*, p. 34.
[3] A white garment worn by the officiants in the synagogue during the service on New Year and Day of Atonement. It is also worn by many individuals at the *Seder* service.
[4] Gamaliel II also called Gamaliel of Javneh.
[5] *Moed Katan* 27b.
[6] *Ibid.*

The *Tachrichim* used to be of different colours such as white or black. Rabbi Jannai, a Palestinian *Amora* of the third century, said to his sons: 'My sons, bury me neither in white shrouds nor in black shrouds. Not in white, lest I do not merit (to be amongst the righteous) and am like a bridegroom among mourners; not in black, in case I have merit and am like a mourner among bridegrooms. But bury me in court garments (mixed colours) that come from overseas.'[1] Rabbi Josiah, on the other hand, gave different instructions: 'Clothe me in white shrouds.'[2] No firm rule concerning shrouds was laid down in early times but from the sixteenth century C.E. it became the general practice to use white shrouds.

THE COFFIN

Coffins used for Jewish funerals must be made of plain unpolished boards without any ornamentation. No metal nails may be used, nor may there be any inside or outside lining. The cover must consist of a single flat board.

The Hebrew word for coffin is *Aron* and although this word occurs many times in the Bible, only in one instance is it used to mean a coffin (Gen. L: 26). In Biblical times coffins were not generally used. Instead the dead were carried to the burial place upon a bed or bier (*Mittah*).

Both in the *Mishnah*[3] and the Talmud[4] there are a number of references to the use of coffins. Rabbi Levi commenting on the verse: 'And Adam and his wife hid themselves from

---

[1] *Shabbat* 114a. Cf. *Midrash* Genesis C. 2, 'Rabbi Jochanan gave instructions before his death: "Do not bury me in white or in black but coloured shrouds, so that if I am summoned with the righteous, the wicked may not be aware of me; while if I am summoned with the wicked, the righteous may not be aware of me." '

[2] Genesis *Rabbah* 100.2.

[3] *Mishnah Eduyot* 5.6.

[4] *Yerushalmi Kilayim* IX.4. Rabbi Judah Hanasi instructed: 'Lower my coffin deep in the earth,' i.e. the board beneath shall be removed so that the coffin shall be in close touch with the earth (*Tur* Y.D. 362).

the presence of the Lord God amongst the trees of the garden' (Gen. III: 8) said, 'This was a sign for his descendants that they would be placed within wooden coffins.'[1]

In mediaeval France it was the practice to use as coffin boards the table upon which food for the poor had been used.

The Cabbalists, on the other hand, took the phrase 'for dust thou art and unto dust shalt thou return' (Gen. III: 19) literally and therefore did not use coffins for burial. This was also the general custom in Eastern Europe before the Nazi holocaust.

In some communities it was customary to place small sticks in the dead person's hands. This custom can be traced to the Palestinian Talmud in which it is recorded that Rabbi Jeremiah requested that a staff be put into his hand when lowered into the grave so that he could be ready to march at the announcement of the coming of the Messiah.[2]

It is forbidden to gain any benefit from either a dead body or the shrouds.[3] Objects which are attached to the body such as a wig or artificial teeth must be interred with the body. However, articles such as ornaments and clothes which are not attached to the body may be used.

FUNERALS ON A HOLY DAY

Funerals may not take place on the Sabbath, or on the Day of Atonement. On the first day of a Festival[4] it was at

---

[1] Genesis *Rabbah* XIX.8.
[2] *Yerushalmi Kilayim* IX.3.
[3] Y.D. 349.
[4] Cf. Code *Orach Chayyim* 526: 'If a body has to be buried on the first day of *Yom Tov*, non-Jews shall perform the labour even if the death occurred on the same day and it would be possible without danger of decomposition to keep the body until the next day. This, however, refers only to the work of making shrouds while the dressing of the body, heating of water for washing it, carrying out the body and placing it in the grave may be carried out by Jews. If one died on the first day of *Yom Tov*, it is permitted to keep the body overnight until the second holy day in order that Jews may perform the services of the funeral.'

one time permitted to hold funerals, provided that certain
functions were performed by Gentiles. On the second day of
a Festival, including the second day of *Rosh Hashanah*,
funerals are permitted and only those whose services are
essential for the burial[1] may ride to the cemetery. The
Rabbis regarded the second day of *Yom Tov* 'as a weekday
as far as the dead are concerned.'[2] It is an accepted custom
in the Anglo-Jewish community not to arrange any funerals
either on the first or second days of *Yom Tov*.

HOME SERVICE PRIOR TO THE FUNERAL

Before the funeral it is usual to recite Psalms and to hold
a brief service in the home. In this connection the late Chief
Rabbi, Dr J. H. Hertz, drew up an Order of Service[3] consisting of Psalms XXIII and CXXX, Scriptural Selections and a
Memorial Prayer, with the plea to God to 'open unto him
(her) the gates of righteousness and light, the gates of pity
and grace. O shelter him (her) for evermore under the
cover of thy wings; and let his (her) soul be bound up in the
bond of eternal life. The Lord is his (her) inheritance; may
he (she) rest in peace. And let us say, Amen.'

[1] i.e. the grave diggers cf. *Mishnah Berurah*, Vol. V, p. 194.
[2] *Bezah* 6a.
[3] A.P.B., pp. 421–23.

43

CHAPTER

IV

THE BET OLAM (House of Eternity)

THE Jewish cemetery has many euphemistic names such as: 'the House of Eternity,' 'Long Home,'[1] 'House of the Living,'[2] 'the Pure Place,' 'the Good Place' (*Guter Ort*). These names spring from the rabbinic belief that this 'world is the temporary lodging place; the world to come is a home.'[3]

BIBLE TIMES

It is difficult to ascertain from the Bible whether there was a generally accepted place of burial. Phrases such as, 'he lay with his fathers,' or 'was gathered unto his fathers,' indicate a preference for burial in family plots or caves. Abraham bought the Cave of Machpelah for four hundred shekels of silver and it became his family sepulchre (Gen. XXIII: 20). There were, however, other types of resting-place in Biblical times. Manasseh, for instance, 'was buried in the garden of his own house' (II Kings XXI: 18); Amon in the garden of Uzza (II Kings XXI: 26); Deborah, Rebeccah's nurse, under an oak tree (Gen. XXXV: 8); Saul under a terebinth tree (I Chron. X: 12); and Rachel on the road near Bethlehem (Gen. XXXV: 19).

Special sepulchres were constructed for the Kings of Judah (II Chron. XXI: 20). There were also communal

---

[1] Eccl. XII: 5.
[2] Cf. Job XXX: 23, 'House appointed for all living.'
[3] *Moed Katan* 9*b*.

burial places, 'the graves of the common people' (II Kings, XXIII: 6, Jer. XXVI: 23).

There are several Biblical references to a desire to be buried together with one's family. Ruth, for example, affirmed: 'Where thou diest, will I die, and there will I be buried' (Ruth I: 17), and Barzillai declined King David's invitation to remain with him at Court, saying: 'Let thy servant, I pray thee, turn back, that I may die in mine own city by the grave of my father and my mother' (II Sam. XIX: 38). Finally, Nehemiah, six centuries later, requested King Artaxerxes to allow him to return from Mesopotamia to the city of his 'father's sepulchres' (Neh. II: 5).

In Talmudic times, burial took place in caves, hewn tombs, stone tombs, sarcophagi and catacombs. Great care was lavished on the cemetery and there was a saying, 'The Jewish graveyards are fairer than royal palaces.'[1]

With the Dispersion, Jewish communities prepared communal cemeteries. Several of these ancient burial places have survived, as for instance the 'Garden Cemetery' of Mayence which dates back to the eleventh century.

It was often difficult for the Jews to obtain their own cemeteries. Until the reign of Henry II there was only one cemetery in the whole of England and it was only in 1177 that each Jewish community was permitted to purchase a place for interring its dead outside the city walls.[2]

Wherever possible the cemetery was situated outside the Jewish quarter, yet near enough to avoid carrying the dead over long distances. Thus in December 1656, within two or three months of renting a house in Creechurch Lane, in the City of London for a Synagogue, the tiny local Jewish community leased a piece of ground in nearby Mile End as a cemetery.[3]

---

[1] *Sanhedrin* 96b.
[2] Cecil Roth, *History of the Jews in England*, p. 13.
[3] Albert M. Hyamson, *The Sephardim of England*, p. 14.

Where Jews were unable to acquire their own exclusive cemetery, they would lease a burial plot from the non-Jewish authorities and they would wherever possible erect a partition which separated the Jewish graves from the others. The Jews planted trees,[1] and took so much care of their cemeteries that a Jewish graveyard often became known as *Hortus Judeorum* (Garden of the Jews).[2]

Even disused cemeteries were carefully preserved and maintained.

DESECRATIONS

It is one of the sad features of Jewish history that not only were Jewish lives always in jeopardy but even the dead were not allowed to rest in peace and there are innumerable records of Jewish cemeteries being desecrated. Pope Calixtus II (1119–24), Eugenius III (1145) and Innocent III (1199) all issued solemn warnings: 'To counteract the wickedness and avarice of evil men in this respect we decree that no one shall dare to desecrate or reduce a Jewish cemetery, or for the sake of gain to exhume human bodies.'[3] Equally stern was the law enacted by Duke Frederick II of Austria on the 1st July, 1244: 'If a Christian attempts to destroy a Jewish cemetery or to break into it, he shall be put to death after the manner of the law, and all his property, no matter what it may be, shall be confiscated by the Duke.'

During the eighteenth century when the 'Resurrectionists' used to plunder graveyards, synagogues instituted a system which ensured a regular guard for the House of Life.

Abraham de Mattos Mocatta (1733–1800) left 200 guineas to have his grave in the burial-ground of the Spanish and Portuguese Jews watched for twelve months.[4]

But the mediaeval acts of desecration pale into insignifi-

[1] Y.D. 368.2.
[2] Israel Abrahams, *Jewish Life in the Middle Ages*, p. 93.
[3] S. W. Baron, *The Jewish Community*, Vol. I, p. 218.
[4] Cecil Roth, *History of the Great Synagogue*, p. 102, note 3.

cance when compared with wholesale systematic destruction of Jewish cemeteries in Europe by the Nazis.

SACRED PLACE

Cemeteries must be treated with respect,[1] and behaviour in them must always be decorous. People must wear suitable head coverings. They may not eat, drink or smoke in a cemetery. Care must be taken not to tread on a grave or lean on a gravestone. It is forbidden to use a path through a cemetery as a short cut. Cattle are not permitted to graze there.[2]

THE MITZVAH OF BURIAL

It was fervently believed that as an act of atonement, the body should be returned as soon as possible to the earth from which it came. Josephus (the Jewish historian of the first century) records that it was forbidden to let anyone lie unburied[3] and thus the burial of a corpse was a sacred duty devolving upon every Jew. Even the High Priest who was forbidden to incur uncleanliness even for his closest relatives was obliged to attend to a *Met Mitzvah*[4] (a corpse which had no one to attend to its burial).

Consideration for the dead is one of the central features of the Book of Tobit and whenever Tobit found an unburied Israelite, he buried him even at the peril of his own life (Tobit II: 8).

Where the primary duty of burial is involved, no distinction may be made between saint and sinner. If there are two bodies to bury, the first to have died must be buried first.[5]

The child of a Jewish mother and a non-Jewish father may be buried in a Jewish cemetery, but Jewish burial is not per-

[1] *Megillah* 29a.
[2] Y.D. 368.1.
[3] *Contra Apion* II.
[4] *Berachot* 19b–20a; *Y.D.* 374.1.
[5] *Y.D.* 354.1.

mitted if the mother is non-Jewish even though the father is Jewish. Non-Jews who have married Jewish women and have not been converted in a recognised *Beth Din* are denied burial in an orthodox Jewish House of Life.

ESCORTING THE DEAD

It is a great *Mitzvah* to escort the dead to their last resting-place. The *Mishnah*[1] lists 'escorting the dead' among the deeds 'the fruit of which a man enjoys in this world while the stock remains for him in the world to come.' So important was this *Mitzvah* considered that our Sages permitted a man to suspend the study of the Torah in order to fulfil it.[2]

'One who sees a funeral procession and does not escort it,' states the Talmud,[3] 'transgresses thereby'. 'Whoso mocketh the poor (i.e. the dead) blasphemeth his Maker' (Prov. XVII: 5) and 'should be placed under a ban.'[4]

Where the dead man is not distinguished for saintliness or scholarship or where there is a great crowd present at the funeral, one may fulfil one's obligation by rising as the funeral cortege passes[5] and escorting it at least four cubits (four paces). In the case of a scholar, however, every effort should be made to accompany the cortege to the cemetery. This old Jewish custom is supported by Josephus who writes: 'All who pass by when a corpse is buried must accompany the funeral and join in the lamentations.'[6]

OBSOLETE RITES

With the passage of time funeral rites have changed considerably. The practice ordered in the *Mishnah*: 'Even

[1] *Peah* I.
[2] *Ketubot* 17a and Y.D. 361.1, 'School children are not suspended from their studies.'
[3] *Berachot* 18a; *Derech Eretz Zuta* IX.
[4] Y.D. 361.3.
[5] *Yerushalmi, Bikkurim* III.3; Y.D. 361.4.
[6] *Contra Apion* II.27.

the poorest man must provide no less than two flute players and one lamenting woman'[1] has been discontinued, as have the use of musical instruments (pipes, harps, tambourines) and the employment of torch bearers and barefooted mourners. In Great Britain, the custom of reciting a formula called *Mechilah* (asking pardon) of the corpse on its arrival at the cemetery was discontinued by Chief Rabbi Nathan Marcus Adler in 1877.[2]

THE BURIAL SERVICE

The coffin is carried into the Hall for the first part of the burial service. The *Zidduk Hadin* (Acknowledgment of the Divine Judgment)[3] begins with the affirmation, 'The Rock, his work is perfect, for all his ways are judgment.'[4]

The prayer originated in Talmudic times and was completed in the Geonic period. Its themes are: resignation and submission to the inscrutable will of God; belief in the immortality of the soul; and the affirmation of the principle that there is a Heavenly judge who will give everyone 'according to his ways and according to the fruit of his doings.'

It concludes with the words: 'The Lord gave and the Lord hath taken away; Blessed be the Name of the Lord. And He being merciful, forgiveth iniquity and destroyeth not; Yea, many a time He turneth His anger away, and doth not stir up all His wrath.'

---

[1] *Ketubot* 46b.

[2] *Laws and Bye-laws of the Burial Society*, p. 13; on the origin of the custom cf. *Yoma* 87a, 'Whosoever offends his neighbour and does it only through words, must pacify him. He should bring ten persons and make them stand by his grave and say: 'I have sinned against the Lord, the God of Israel and against this one whom I have hurt.'

[3] In many communities *Zidduk Hadin* is recited after the coffin has been lowered into the grave.

[4] A.P.B., pp. 424–5.

On those days on which *Tachanun* is not said, Psalm xvi[1] is read instead of this prayer. *Zidduk Hadin* is not recited on Friday afternoon or on the eve of a Festival. It is, however, recited on the eve of the New Moon, on the eve of *Purim* and on the eve of *Chanukah*.[2] On the days after the New Moon of *Sivan* until Pentecost, on the 9th of *Av* and on the eve of New Year, it should be said before noon.[3]

The coffin is then borne from the *Ohel* (hall) to the grave. In Talmudic times during the funeral procession it was the custom to stop seven times and make lamentations over the dead.[4] It is still customary to halt several times[5] (at least three times) on the way to the grave when Psalm xci is recited.[6] The customary halts are not made at the cemetery on days when *Zidduk Hadin* is not recited.

The seven halts are symbolic of the seven times the word *Hevel* (Vanity) occurs in the Book of Ecclesiastes.[7] The number seven, too, corresponds to the days of the world's creation and also to the seven stages which man experiences in his lifetime.[8]

When the coffin is lowered into the grave all those who are present say: 'May he (or she) come to his (or her) place in peace.'[9]

It is a *Mitzvah* to fill the grave. Three spadesful[10] of earth are dropped into the grave by those present as a symbol of the three-fold composition of man: soul, spirit and breath. After the spade has been used it must not be passed to the

[1] Y.D. 401.6 (*Rema*).
[2] *Kitzur Shulchan Aruch* 198.14; Greenwald, *op. cit.* p. 211.
[3] *Ibid.*
[4] *Mishnah, Ketubot* 2.10; *Baba Batra* 6.7; *Oholot* 18.4; *Baba Batra* 100b.
[5] Y.D. 358.3 (*Rema*).
[6] A.P.B., p. 24.
[7] Eccl. 1: 2; *Baba Batra* 100b.
[8] Eccl. *Rabbah* 1: 1.
[9] A.P.B., p. 427.
[10] *Maavar Yabok* mentions five spadesful.

next man but replaced on the ground so that one man should not appear to be passing on trouble to another. Moreover, the passing of the spade from hand to hand would indicate overlordship and servitude attitudes, but in the presence of death all are equal. 'Neither hath he power over the day of death' (Eccl. VIII: 8).

WASHING THE HANDS

When the grave is filled the mourners and all those present at the funeral wash their hands[1] and say: 'He maketh death to vanish in life eternal; and the Lord God wipeth away tears from off all faces; and the reproach of his people shall he take away from off all the earth: for the Lord hath spoken it.'[2]

One of the many reasons given for this custom is that it may be a symbolic demonstration that there is no responsibility for the death of the deceased.[3]

The mourners return to the Hall and Psalm XCI[4] is then recited preceded by the last verse of Psalm XC. This is followed by the *Kaddish*[5] and a Memorial Prayer.[6] Two rows are formed between which the mourners pass and those present say to the mourners the words: 'May the Almighty comfort you among the other mourners for Zion and Jerusalem.'[7]

The custom of 'passing through two parallel rows of friends,' too, is of Talmudic origin.[8] 'Formerly the mourners used to stand still,' records the Talmud,[9] 'while the people

[1] Y.D. 376.4.
[2] A.P.B., p. 427.
[3] Deut. XXI: 7. Some people do not dry their hands with a towel so not to seem to wish to wipe off the memory of the deceased.
[4] A.P.B., p. 24.
[5] *Ibid*, pp. 428–9.
[6] *Ibid*, pp. 431–3.
[7] *Ibid*, p. 147.
[8] *Yerushalmi Berachot* 3.2; *Megillah* 23b *Rashi*; *Baba Batra* 100b.
[9] *Sanhedrin* 19a.

passed by. But there were families in Jerusalem which contended with one another, each maintaining, "We shall pass first," so the Rabbis established the rule that the public should remain standing and the mourners pass by.'

PLUCKING GRASS

On leaving the burial ground it is customary to pluck a few blades of grass[1] and say: 'And may they blossom out of the city like grass of the earth' (Ps. LXXII: 16) or 'He remembereth that we are dust (Ps. CIII: 14). This custom is an allusion to the resurrection of the dead.

There is no *din* governing the attendance of women at funerals. It is a question of local custom as to whether they attend and in Anglo-Jewry women are discouraged from attending. In Germany, on the other hand, it was not unusual for women to attend funerals.[2]

FLOWERS

Flowers played an important part in the idolatrous rites of many ancient peoples. They were sprinkled on the marriage bed, on the altar, and on the grave. The placing of flowers on the grave is therefore regarded as *Chukat Hagoy* (pagan custom) and it is discouraged by Orthodox rabbinic authorities. Yet there are many references in the Talmud[3] to spices for the dead. Rabbi Jannai commanded his sons to place myrtle twigs on his body and it was even permitted to cut myrtle twigs on the second day of the festival for this purpose.[4]

MEMORIAL ADDRESS

It is regarded as unnatural not to weep for the dead. 'My son,' says Ben Sira, 'let thy tears fall over the dead, and as

[1] Y.D. 376.4.
[2] The *Zohar* (*Vayakhal* 196b) strongly disapproves: 'For when the women wail in the funeral procession, the Angel of Death descends and places himself among them.'
[3] *Berachot* 53a; *Baba Kamma* 16b.
[4] *Bezah* 6a and *Orach Chayyim* 526.4.

one that suffereth grievously begin lamentation . . . Make bitter weeping and make passionate wailing, and let thy mourning be according to his desert, for one day or two, lest thou be evil spoken of; and so be comforted for thy sorrow' (Eccl. XXXVIII: 16–18). The Bible also records David's moving eulogies when he mourned over Saul, Jonathan and Abner. There were even professional mourners[1] whose bitter lamentations were an example for the mourners. 'Call for the mourning women, that they may come; and send for the wise women, that they may come' (Jer. IX: 16). Often they used a set refrain: 'Alas, my brother!' or 'Ah Lord!' (I Kings XII: 30; Jer. XXXIV: 5).

Our Sages, too, stress the importance of lamentation at funerals.[2] The *Hesped*[3] (Memorial Address) is delivered before the interment, either in the house or at the cemetery. It is forbidden to praise the dead too highly or attribute to them qualities that they did not possess. A body should not be taken into the synagogue for the *Hesped*, except in the case of a noted rabbinical scholar or a man of exemplary piety.

EXHUMATION

Jewish tradition forbids exhumation, because this is considered disrespectful. Exception is made, however, in certain circumstances,[4] such as when the remains are to be transported to the Holy Land, for 'whoever is buried in the land of Israel,' says the Talmud,[5] 'is deemed to be buried, under the Altar.'

Atoning power of the earth was attributed to the Holy

---

[1] *Mishnah Moed Katan* III.8.

[2] Rav urged Samuel ben Shelat: 'Deliver an oration for I shall surely be there to hear your words.' *Shabbat* 153a; *Moed Katan 8a* and 25b; *Yerushalmi, Ketubot* XII.3.

[3] Lit. 'To strike, to beat,' cf. Isa. XXXII: 12, 'Smiting upon the breasts.'

[4] *Mishnah Baba Batra* II.9; *Semachot* XIV; *Tosephta Baba Batra* I.1.

[5] *Ketubot* 111a.

Land[1] and burial there was a sure means of expiation. Moreover, the resurrection is expected to take place in the Holy Land. Those who have died in the Diaspora, runs the legend, will roll across the earth through cavities until they reach the Holy Land,[2] where they will be brought back to life. In the words of the Sages,[3] 'Why did the Patriarchs deserve to be buried in *Eretz Israel*? (Land of Israel). Because the dead of *Eretz Israel* will be the first to be revived in the Messianic period and to enter the year of Messianic splendour.'

A Jewish body buried in a non-Jewish cemetery may be exhumed in order to be re-interred in a Jewish House of Life. In Britain, the Burial Society insists that 'no exhumation shall take place except in accordance with the procedure laid down by Her Majesty's Principal Secretary of State, and with the prior approval of the Chief Rabbi.'[4]

---

[1] Deut. xxxii: 43: 'The earth shall atone for his people.'
[2] *Ketubot* 111a.
[3] *Tanchumah* Genesis, *Vayyechi* (ed. Buber Vilna, 1885), p. 214.
[4] *Laws and Bye-laws of the Burial Society*, p. 102 (Q.3).

CHAPTER

V

THE SHIVAH—A UNIQUE INSTITUTION

IMMEDIATELY after the funeral the bereaved family gather together in the house of the deceased to sit *Shivah* (lit. seven) and this they do for seven days. During this period they sit on low stools and are prohibited from performing manual labour or conducting business transactions, bathing or anointing the body, cohabitation, washing and preparing garments, cutting the hair. Torah study excepting that of certain portions of the Scriptures and of other sacred works is also forbidden.

Morning (*Shacharit*), Afternoon (*Minchah*) and Evening (*Maariv*) services are held in the house.

The *Shivah* is a unique institution. For seven days, the mourners, irrespective of status or disposition, are united in their common sorrow. Daily routine and work cease. Death, with its awesome majesty, casts its shadow on the mourners.

Most of the *Shivah* customs which developed in Talmudic times have been retained although a number of them, such as wearing sackcloth and sitting in ashes, have been discarded.

The Sages offer a number of reasons why seven has been chosen as the period of mourning. One teacher, commenting on the verse 'I will turn your feasts into mourning' (Amos VIII: 10) says, 'Just as the days of the Feasts (Passover and Tabernacles) are seven, so are the days of mourning.'[1] Another teacher traces it back to the verse: 'Let her not, I

---

[1] *Moed Katan* 20a; *Yerushalmi Moed Katan* 3.5.

55

pray, be as one dead . . . And Miriam was shut up without the camp seven days' (Num. XII: 12–15); the days of isolation (for leprosy) are seven (Lev. XIII: 31); finally, the *Zohar* gives a mystical reason: 'For seven days the soul goes to and fro, from the house to the grave and from the grave to the house, mourning for the body.'[1]

The antiquity of the *Shivah* is unquestioned. Our Sages, in fact, maintain that this institution is even older than the Flood. 'And it came to pass after the seven days, that the waters of the flood were upon the earth' (Gen. VII: 10). 'What was the nature of these seven days?' asks the Talmud.[2] 'These were the days of mourning for Methuselah, thus teaching that the lamentation for the righteous postpones retribution.' 'God Himself,' attests Rabbi Joshua ben Levi (a third-century Amora), 'mourned seven days for the destruction of the world.'

In patriarchal times the 'seven days'[3] are first mentioned in connection with Jacob, when it is stated that Joseph 'made a mourning for his father seven days' (Gen. L: 10). According to the Palestinian Talmud, it was Moses who appointed seven days of mourning.[4] The Apocrypha is very explicit on this point. Ben Sira declares: 'Seven days are the days of mourning for the dead' (XXII: 12).

The day of burial counts as the first day of the *Shivah* provided the interment was completed before sunset and the *Shivah* ends on the morning of the seventh day. On that day the mourners fulfil their obligations by sitting for a short while (one hour). When the seventh day falls on the Sabbath, the mourner does not resume his *Shivah*, which in this case ends with the conclusion of the morning service. The Sabbath is included in the Seven Days of Mourning although no outward signs of mourning apply on that day.

On Friday, or on the eve of a Festival (unless it is on the

[1] *Vayyechi* 26a.
[2] *Sanhedrin* 108b.
[3] *Yerushalmi Moed Katan* 3.5.
[4] *Ketubot* 1.1.

seventh day when one hour suffices), mourning is observed until two and a half hours prior to nightfall. An exception is made on Passover Eve when mourning ends at noon.

Shivah must be observed for father, mother, wife, husband, son, daughter, brother and sister (including half-brother and half-sister) but not for an infant less than thirty days old. From the age of thirteen and one day (in the case of boys) and twelve and one day (in the case of girls), children must observe the laws of mourning for their relatives.

A mourner who has been prevented by sickness from observing the *Shivah* must do so on his recovery, if by then the thirty days have not elapsed since death.

Because of the injunction: 'And thou shalt rejoice in thy Feast' (Deut. XVI: 14) our Rabbis deduced that a Festival annuls the *Shivah*, provided that the mourner has been able to observe the *Shivah* one hour before the commencement of the festival.[1] The New Year and the Day of Atonement, although not characterised by rejoicing, terminates the *Shivah*,[2] since these two Festivals are included in the 'appointed season' mentioned in Lev. XXIII: 4, 'These are the appointed seasons of the Lord, even holy convocations, which ye shall proclaim in their appointed season.'

If the deceased leaves instructions that his relatives should not observe *Shivah*, his wishes must be disregarded.

A telegram may be accepted as a *bona fide* evidence of death, thus requiring the relative to observe *Shivah*. In the case of a missing person or one presumed drowned, the relatives do not observe mourning unless there is evidence of death.

SEUDAT HAVRA'AH (MEAL OF CONSOLATION)

The mourner's first meal after the funeral is known as *Seudat Havra'ah* (Meal of Consolation). This meal is invariably provided by friends and neighbours in obedience

[1] Y.D. 399.1.
[2] *Mishnah Moed Katan* 19*a*; Y.D. 399.6.

to the Talmudic injunction, 'A mourner is forbidden to eat of his own food at the first meal after the burial.'[1] Reference to this custom is made by both Jeremiah and Ezekiel. 'Neither shall men break bread for them in mourning, to comfort for the dead; neither shall men give them the cup of consolation to drink for their father or for their mother' (Jer. XVI: 7). Ezekiel was told by God, 'Sigh in silence; make no mourning for the dead, bind thy headtire upon thee, and put thy shoes upon thy feet, and cover not thine upper lip, and eat not the bread of men' (XXIV: 17). Ezekiel was forbidden to observe the practices of mourning. We see therefore that one of the rites of mourning was not to eat of one's own food but to allow others to provide food. This custom gives friends and neighbours the opportunity to express in a practical form their solicitude and sympathy.

The Talmud[2] tells how, in ancient times, it was the custom to take food to a house of mourning. For the rich, food was conveyed in baskets of gold and silver; for the poor in baskets of osier willows. As this made the poor feel ashamed, the Rabbis ruled that willow baskets should be used to convey the food to all mourners, rich and poor alike.

The menu of this meal has changed from that of Talmudic times[3] and according to the tradition followed nowadays it consists of hard-boiled eggs and rolls of bread. These have a special symbolism. In ancient times, the egg was regarded as a symbol of life and resurrection. Moreover, because the egg is completely sealed inside its shell, it serves as a reminder to the mourners to remain silent and refrain from casual talk. Bread of course, is the staple food, for it 'stayeth man's heart' (Ps. CIV: 15).

---

[1] *Moed Katan* 27b; Y.D. 378.1.

[2] *Moed Katan*, 27a.

[3] *Ketubot* 8b: Following the Scriptural precept, 'Give strong drink unto him that is ready to perish, and wine unto the bitter in soul' (Prov. XXXI: 6–7), the Rabbis ordered ten cups of wine to be served with the 'meal of consolation.' 'Wine was created,' declared Rabbi Chanan, 'for the sole purpose of consoling the bereaved.' *Sanhedrin* 70a.

It was also customary to provide the mourners with lentils because, the Rabbis said, they were made into a broth by Jacob to comfort his father when Abraham died.[1] Our Sages gave an additional reason, *viz.* 'Lentils are round like a wheel and mourning is a revolving wheel that touches everyone sooner or later.' Yet a further reason is that just as lentils have no mouths, so too must mourners 'have no mouth,' for they are forbidden to greet people.[2]

Salt is not placed on the table. Normally, it is usual to dip bread in salt because the table is compared to a sacrificial altar, and the Bible says of sacrifice: 'And every meal offering of thine shalt thou season with salt' (Lev. II: 13). Since a mourner may not offer a sacrifice there can be no place for salt on his table.

If burial takes place on Friday afternoon, the mourner should not be served with a Meal of Condolence[3] nor is it obligatory for the Meal to be served at the termination of the Sabbath. On *Chol Hamoed*[4] (the half festive days intervening between the last days of Passover and *Sukkot*), on *Purim, Chanukah* and *Rosh Chodesh* (New Moon) it is prepared, but not on the eve of Passover, so that the mourner's relish for the unleavened bread at the *Seder* should not be diminished. The *Seudat Havra'ah* is not served if the news of a death arrives after thirty days.[5] Nor is the meal served if the mourner wishes to fast after the funeral till nightfall.

Candles must burn continuously for the entire seven days.[6]

---

[1] *Baba Batra* 16*b*; Y.D. 378.9.
[2] *Midrash* Genesis *Rabbah* 63.14.
[3] Y.D. 378.5.
[4] Only if the burial took place on *Chol Hamoed*. The mourner must eat it while sitting at the table for there is no mourning on *Chol Hamoed*. *Kitzur Shulchan Aruch* 205.8. Cf. *Talmudic Encyclopaedia*, Vol. VIII, p. 146, note III.
[5] *Tosaphot Moed Katan* 24*b*; *Tur Shulchan Aruch* 278; *Yerushalmi Moed Katan* III.5. Y.D. 378.12.
[6] *Nachalat Shivah* 73. It was also customary to keep a glass of water and a towel during the *Shivah*. Rabbi Abraham Danzig in *Chochmat Adom* (p. 461), disapproves of this *Minhag*.

Before his death, Rabbi Judah Hanasi (135–219) instructed that a light should be kept burning in his home[1] and the custom was widely practised as early as the thirteenth century.

LOW STOOLS

In earlier times people normally sat on couches or beds. During the period of mourning they were required to overturn them[2] and sit on the ground. There is Biblical authority for this. When King David became a mourner, he 'lay on the earth (II Sam. XIII: 31). And it states in the Book of Job: 'So they sat down with him upon the ground seven days and seven nights' (Job II: 13).

Nowadays, it is customary for the mourners to sit on low stools.

The mourner is not allowed to put on leather footwear;[3] he must wear slippers of cloth, felt or rubber. This does not apply to a woman after confinement,[4] an expectant mother or someone with an injured foot.[5] An invalid whose health may be injured by going without shoes, is permitted to wear them. The other exception is that when the mourner leaves the house (for instance to attend the Synagogue on the Sabbath) he may wear leather shoes. A mourner who walks out of doors is permitted to wear boots. He should, however, sprinkle a little earth therein.

BATHING

The mourner is forbidden to bathe all over even in cold water.[6] This prohibition is based on the verse in the second Book of Samuel (XVI: 2), 'And Joab sent to Tekoa, and fetched thence a wise woman, and said to her: "I pray thee, feign thyself to be a mourner, and put on mourning apparel, I pray thee, and anoint not thyself with oil." '

[1] *Ketubot* 103a.
[2] *Moed Katan* 15a–b; Y.D. 378.1.
[3] Y.D. 380.1 and 382.1; *Moed Katan* 15b.
[4] Y.D. 382.2.
[5] *Orach Chayyim* 614.3.
[6] *Moed Katan* 15b; Y.D. 381.1.

Bathing, like anointing, is included among the pleasures forbidden to mourners, who may, however, wash their faces, hands and feet in cold water.[1] The prohibition against bathing is waived for a man covered with mud, a woman after childbirth, or a delicate person[2] who must bathe himself for reasons of health.

A woman should not use any cosmetics during the *Shivah*[3] period. A more lenient attitude is adopted in this respect towards a bride or a young girl.

The Talmud[4] relates that services were held in the house of the mourner. When a neighbour of Rabbi Judah died without there being any surviving children to be comforted, the Rabbi assembled ten men daily and offered prayers in his memory. The dead man appeared to the Rabbi in a dream and said: 'Thy mind be at rest, for thou hast set my mind at rest.'

Praying in the house of mourners so as to show respect for both the dead and the living was a well-established custom in the Middle Ages. One of the functions of the *Hebra Maarib beZemanah Oheb Shalom*, founded in 1790 in London, was to provide a *minyan*[5] during the *Shivah*.[6]

In 1853 *Hebrath Menachem Abelim Hesed Ve Emeth* ('Society of kindness and for comforting the mourners') was formed in London. In return for a weekly contribution of two pence the friendly society undertook to provide:

1. A *Shivah* benefit of ten shillings during the week of confined mourning.
2. *Minyan* during *Shivah*.

---

[1] Y.D. 381.1.
[2] '*Rabban* Gamaliel washed himself the first night of his wife's death. His disciples said to him: "Master, didst thou not teach us that a mourner is forbidden to wash himself?" He replied "I am not in this respect like other men. I am of delicate health." ' *Berachot* 2.6; Y.D. 381.3.
[3] Y.D. 381.6.
[4] *Shabbat* 152a.
[5] Lit. number or quorum: Ten men above the age of 13.
[6] Cecil Roth, *The History of the Great Synagogue*, p. 61, n. 11.

3. Payment of a Rabbi to speak at morning and evening service at *Shivah* and on the Sabbath of the *Sheloshim*.[1]

A *Sepher Torah* for the Reading of the Law during the Services should be loaned by the Community if proper facilities for its care are available and also providing it is to be read on three occasions.

If it is not possible to obtain a *minyan* in the home, the mourner in certain circumstances may go to the Synagogue for Services.

LITURGY

In the house of mourning, the normal order of the Daily Services is subject to variations. The additions, substitutions and omissions are as follows:

1. Psalm XLIX[2] (which expresses firm belief in the Redemption of the Soul) is read.
2. The Talmudical passage *Pitum Haketoret*[3] ('The compound forming incense') is omitted.
3. *Tachanun* (Petitions of Grace), also known as *Nephilat Appayim* (falling on the face),[4] are omitted. The theme of *Tachanun* is 'I have sinned before Thee' and is deemed inappropriate to a mourner.
4. On those days on which *Tachanun* is not said, Psalm XVI[5] (which praises complete submission to the Divine Will) is substituted for Psalm XLIV.
5. Psalm XX[6] is omitted.
6. The Priestly Benediction[7] (Num. VI: 24–26) is omitted.

---

[1] V. D. Lipman, *Social History of the Jews in England, 1850–1950*. London, 1954, p. 72.
[2] A.P.B., pp. 429–30.
[3] *Keritot 6a*; A.P.B., pp. 219–220.
[4] A.P.B. pp.60–68.
[5] *Ibid*, p. 426.
[6] *Ibid*, pp. 75–6.
[7] *Ibid*, pp. 5 and 55.

7. The mourner omits the six Psalms (xcv–xcix and xxix) recited before the Evening Service on Friday night.

   At the Synagogue on Friday evening mourners remain in the ante-room until the conclusion of *Lechah Dodi* ('Come, my friend).

   The beadle then announces: 'Comfort the mourners,' and the congregation rises and greets them with the words: 'May the Almighty comfort you among the other mourners for Zion and Jerusalem.'[1]

8. The verse (Psalm xc: 17) 'And let the graciousness of the Lord our God be upon us: establish thou also upon us the work of our hands, yea, the work of our hands establish thou it' is omitted.[2]

9. Spices are not used for the *Havdalah* Service (the benedictions recited at the termination of the Sabbath) in the house of a mourner.[3]

10. In the Grace After Meals, the passage: 'Comfort, O Lord our God, the mourners of Jerusalem' is substituted for the verse, 'And rebuild Jerusalem, the holy city, speedily in our days.'[4]

11. *Hallel* ('Hymns of Praise' Psalms cxiii–cxviii) is not said in the house of a mourner on *Rosh Chodesh* and *Chanukah*[5] because they contain sentiments which might sadden mourners, such as, 'The dead praise not the Lord, neither any that go down into silence (Psalm cxv: 17) and, 'This is the day which the Lord hath made, we will rejoice and be glad in it' (Psalm cxviii: 24). If possible, the mourner should go into another room while the congregation recite the *Hallel*.

---

[1] *Ibid*, p. 147.

[2] Greenwald, *op cit*. p. 281.

[3] *Ibid*, pp. 282 and 370. Some authorities permit the use of spices.

[4] A.P.B., pp. 380–1.

[5] Some authorities maintain that on *Chanukah*, *Hallel* should be recited with the congregation even in the house of a mourner.

If *Rosh Chodesh* occurs on the Sabbath, *Hallel* should be recited with the congregation even in the house of a mourner, for on the Sabbath there is no outward mourning.

12. The mourner is not called up to the Reading of the Law during the week of *Shivah* even if he is the only Cohen or Levi in the congregation.

13. In the *Kaddish Shalem* though, the words, 'May the Prayers of all Israel be accepted by their Father who is in heaven'[1] are not said by the mourner himself; they are generally recited by the officiating reader in the House of Mourning.

TEPHILLIN ON THE FIRST DAY

The Code states:[2] 'On the first day of the *Shivah*, mourners do not put on *Tephillin*.[3] This is deduced from the Divine Command to Ezekiel who, when he became a mourner, was instructed 'to bind thy headtire upon thee' (Ezek. XXIV: 17), i.e. *Tephillin*, the implication being that all other mourners are exempt from putting on *Tephillin* on the first day as they must not indulge in any personal adornment. This view has been endorsed by many leading rabbinical authorities, among them Rabbi David b. Samuel Halevi, the *Taz*, Joseph ben Meir Teomin (1727–1793) and Rabbi Akiva Eger (1761–1837).

The custom nowadays is to put on *Tephillin* on the first day of the *Shivah*, though some authorities maintain that the mourner need not make the usual benedictions.

If, however, burial took place at twilight and the mourner immediately commenced his *Shivah*, the authorities hold that he should put on the *Tephillin* the following day, since this was considered as the second day of mourning. A man

[1] A.P.B., p. 79.
[2] Y.D. 380.1; 388.1; *Moed Katan* 15a.
[3] Phylacteries; small cases containing passages from the Scriptures and affixed to the forehead and arm during the recital of prayers (Deut. VI: 8).

bereaved on *Chol Hamoed* should put on *Tephillin* provided that it is his practice to put on *Tephillin* on those days.

A mourner is permitted to conduct services in his own house since he is bound to observe all the *Mitzvot*. If a person mourning for his parents officiates in the Synagogue he complies with the usual order of the service[1] including the recital of the Priestly Benediction, but he omits *Tachanun*. He should not officiate on *Rosh Chodesh* nor on days when *Tachanun* is not said. He may go to the Synagogue to hear the *Megillah* on *Purim* but must not himself recite the *Megillah* for the congregation. From *Rosh Chodesh Elul* till after *Yom Kippur* and during the Ten Days of Penitence, the mourner may officiate and may even recite *Selichot*.

During the *Shivah* week a mourner should not officiate as Reader on the Sabbath and Festivals unless there is no one else to do so.

A mourner during the *Shivah* period should not go from his house to the Synagogue to recite *Selichot* except on the eve of *Rosh Hashanah* when many *Selichot* are said.[2]

In times of pestilence, one does not observe mourning rites;[3] 'I have heard,' confirms Rabbi Moses Isserles, 'that some have adopted this practice.'[4]

If a mourner is prevented through illness from commencing the period of the *Shivah* at the time of the interment, he is not required to observe the full seven days on his recovery but must observe the remaining days of the *Shivah*.

---

[1] If there be a mourner at the Synagogue, the congregation does not in this respect do as he does and they have to say *Tachanum* while the mourner himself need not say it. *Kitzur Shulchan Aruch* 22.5.

[2] *Ibid*, 128.10.

[3] Y.D. 374.11 (*Rema*).

[4] *Ibid*, 374.11.

CHAPTER

VI

THE MANNER OF MOURNING

JUDAISM makes many demands of mourners and all with good reason. The mourning period is ordered, not to enforce idleness or encourage morbid thought, but for reflection and self-examination. During these few brief days, all normal activities are suspended.

For the period of the *Shivah*, as has already been mentioned, the mourner is forbidden to do any work or even to supervise work that is performed by others, whether they be fellow-Jews or Gentiles.

In certain exceptional circumstances, such as poverty or where irreparable loss is probable, the mourner, after consulting a Rabbi, may be permitted to carry on his usual work after the third day of the *Shivah*. Nevertheless, our Sages say: 'May a curse come upon his neighbours who [by not providing for his maintenance] force the mourner to work.'[1]

It is regarded as a great *Mitzvah* to give alms to poor people during the *Shivah*.

Although the Law in general requires total cessation from any gainful occupation by a mourner during the *Shivah*, it makes a number of important concessions. It is permitted to delegate to others the execution of transactions which if postponed would entailed irretrievable loss. Such transactions include the recovery of debts, receiving com-

[1] *Yerushalmi, Moed Katan* 111.5.

missions for work to be executed later and the writing of urgent letters.[1]

If two individuals own a shop in partnership and one of them becomes a mourner, the shop should be closed.[2] Where, however, great loss may result, rabbinical authorities should be consulted as to whether it may be opened after three days.

It is permissible for a woman in mourning to bake and cook and attend to all her domestic duties.[3] Sweeping the house, washing up and making the beds are not considered forbidden work for the mourner.[4] A domestic servant may carry out her normal duties during the period of the *Shivah*. She must not, however, leave the house during the *Shivah*.

STUDY

The Psalmist says: 'The precepts of the Lord are right, rejoicing the heart' (Ps. xix: 9). Our Rabbis have therefore forbidden a mourner to study or even to meditate on the Pentateuch, Prophets, Hagiographa, *Mishnah*, *Talmud*, *Halachot* or *Aggadot*.[5] Both Ezekiel and Job throw light on this command. 'Sigh in silence' says the former (Ezek. xxiv: 17), and 'None spoke a word' (in Job ii: 13) have been homiletically explained as 'Torah Study.'[6]

However, the mourner may spend his time reading the following works: the Book of Job, Lamentations, the sad parts of Jeremiah,[7] the chapter *Eilu Megalchin*[8] (which deals with the laws concerning mourning and excommunication),

---

[1] i.e. such writing as is permitted on *Chol Hamoed*.
[2] Y.D. 380.21.
[3] *Ibid*, 22.
[4] *Semachot* xi.9 and *Moed Katan* 27a.
[5] *Halachot*—The Law, the legal literature of the Jew. *Aggadot*—Ethical or homiletical portions of rabbinic literature. *Moed Katan* 21a; Y.D. 384.1.
[6] *Yerushalmi Moed Katan* iii.5. In the name of Rabbi Yochanan.
[7] Y.D. 384.4.
[8] *Moed Katan*, Chapter iii.

tractate *Semachot*,[1] *Menorat Hamoor* ('Candelabrum of Light') by Rabbi Isaac Aboab the Elder, a religio-ethical writer of the fourteenth century.

GREETINGS

During the first three days of the *Shivah* the mourner does not greet people or reply to them,[2] as this period is devoted to strict mourning. After the third day, the mourner may reply to those who greet him.

This custom, too, like so many of the mourning rites, is derived from Ezekiel who was told 'Sigh in silence' (XXIV: 17).

After the *Shivah*, but before the end of the *Sheloshim*, the mourner may greet others but these do not return the greeting of peace.[3] According to Rabbi Zechariah Mendel the *Baer Hetev*, conventional salutations like 'Good morning' and 'Good day' are not included in the prohibition which is confined to the *Shalom Aleichem* (Peace be unto you) formula.

It is permissible to greet mourners on Sabbath.[4] The Talmud relates that on one occasion Rabbi Hoshaya, the Elder, went to a certain place and met mourners on the Sabbath. He greeted them by saying: 'I know not what is the custom of your place [with regard to greeting on the Sabbath]; however, peace be unto you in accordance with the custom of your place.'[5]

COMFORTING THE MOURNERS

It is a great *Mitzvah* to comfort the mourners. 'It is one of those things,' say the Rabbis, 'that brings good to the world.'[6] God Himself comforted the mourners in one in-

[1] Lit. 'Joyful Occasions.' A minor tractate of the *Talmud* which deals with death and mourning customs.

[2] *Moed Katan* 15a; Y.D. 385.1.

[3] *Ibid*, 385.1.

[4] Maimonides *Yad Evel* x.1; cf. Y.D. 385.3.

[5] *Yerushalmi Moed Katan* III.5.

[6] *Avot de Rabbi Nathan* xxx (ed. Schechter), p. 45.

stance:[1] 'And it came to pass after the death of Abraham, that God blessed Isaac his son' (Gen. xxv: 11). According to Ecclesiastes (vii: 2), 'It is better to go to the house of mourning, than to go to the house of feasting.' The *Midrash* illustrates this idea with the parable: 'It is as if there were two ocean-going ships, one leaving the harbour and the other entering it. As the one sailed out of the harbour the bystanders all rejoiced, but none displayed any joy over the one which was entering the harbour. A wise man was there and he said to the people: "I take the opposite view to you. There is no cause to rejoice over the ship which is leaving the harbour because nobody knows what will be its plight, what seas and storms it may encounter; but when it enters the harbour all have occasion to rejoice since it has come in safely." Similarly when a person dies all should rejoice and offer thanks that he departed from the world with a good name and in peace.'[2]

In both the Bible and Rabbinic literature there are many references to visiting the bereaved. We read in the Bible how Jacob was consoled by his children: 'And all his sons and all his daughters rose up to comfort him' (Gen. xxxvii: 35). According to the Talmud both Ahab and Elijah went to comfort Hiel, the Bethelite, when his sons died (I Kings xvi: 34).[3] Similarly, the *Tannaim*[4] and the *Amoraim*[5] used to visit bereaved teachers, colleagues and disciples and console them.[6]

The manner of visiting a mourner is as important as the visit itself. Respect should be shown for the mourner's grief and bitterness. Indeed, the danger of converting the *Shivah* visit into a social occasion was not unknown to the Rabbis.

---

[1] *Sotah* 14a.
[2] Ecclesiastes *Rabbah* vii.4 in the name of Rabbi Phineas.
[3] *Sanhedrin* 113a.
[4] Teachers quoted in the *Mishnah* or *Beraita*.
[5] The name given to the rabbinic authorities responsible for the *Gemara*.
[6] *Moed Katan* 28b; 21b.

'The merit of attending a house of mourning,' says the Talmud, 'lies in the silence observed.'[1]

Throughout the ages discreet men, like Job's comforters, paid their visits of condolence in sympathetic silence. 'So they sat down with him upon the ground seven days and seven nights, and none spoke a word unto him; for they saw that his grief was very great' (Job II: 13). Also, when Aaron was bereaved, he 'held his peace' (Lev. x: 3). In general, visitors are advised not to speak until the mourner has spoken.

The present-day practice of sending or bringing gifts of food to the mourner during the *Shivah* is frowned on by many Rabbinical authorities, since this is regarded as copying the Gentiles. A distinction, however, is made between necessities which may be sent, and luxuries such as cakes and sweets, which should not be sent. Basically, gifts are not approved of because they might bring joy and thus lessen the natural sorrow which the mourner feels.

The *Mitzvah* of comforting the mourner cannot be fulfilled by telephone since the would-be comforter cannot be deemed to have participated personally in the act.

Upon leaving, the visitor should approach the mourner and say:

הַמָּקוֹם יְנַחֵם אֶתְכֶם בְּתוֹךְ שְׁאָר אֲבֵלֵי צִיּוֹן וִירוּשָׁלָיִם:

'May the Almighty comfort you among the other mourners for Zion and Jerusalem.'

LAUNDERED GARMENTS

The mourner is not allowed to wash his garments during the *Shivah*, because this involves work, which is forbidden.[2] Therefore he must wear only garments that were washed prior to the *Shivah*. A reference to this is found in the Second Book of Samuel (XIV: 2): 'I pray thee, feign thyself to be a mourner, and put on mourning apparel, I pray thee,

[1] *Berachot 6b.*
[2] Y.D. 389: 1.

and anoint not thyself with oil, but be as a woman that had a long time mourned for the dead.'

It is likewise forbidden to wash household linen.[1] On the Sabbath the tables may be covered with clean table-cloths provided that they were washed before the *Shivah*.

A mourner may not have his hair cut, shave his beard[2] or cut his finger nails. 'Let not the hair of your heads go loose' (Lev. x: 6), the mourning Priests were commanded in the tabernacle. The interpretation of this is that all other mourners must let their hair grow long during the *Shivah*. They are, however, permitted to comb it.[3]

There is 'a time to weep, and a time to laugh,' says Ecclesiastes (III: 4). But although only the first three days are designated as 'days of weeping' any kind of entertainment is strictly forbidden during the *Shivah*.

If the mourner celebrates a *Brit Milah* (circumcision) during the *Shivah*, he may change his clothes and go to the Synagogue but may not cut his hair. Neither may he provide a festive meal,[4] though he may invite ten people in order to recite the special Grace After Meals. If there is no one else available he may act as the *Mohel*.[5] After the third day he may also act as *Gevater* (one who carries the infant) or *Sandek* (the man who holds the baby on his knees during the circumcision), but he must not participate in the *Seudah* (Feast) afterwards. Nor may he join in a *Seudah* on the occasion of the Redemption of a first-born or the conclusion of a Talmudic tractate. He may not in any circumstances attend a wedding feast, even if it takes place in his own house. Nor may he leave his home to hear the seven marriage benedictions.[6]

[1] Y.D. 389.1.
[2] *Moed Katan* 14*a*; Y.D. 390.1.
[3] *Ibid*, s. 6.
[4] *Ibid*, 391.3.
[5] *Ibid*, 393.4 *Rema*: 'In every matter connected with a religious duty that cannot be performed without the mourner, he is permitted to go out in order to perform the *Mitzvah*.'
[6] Y.D. 393.2.

It is forbidden to have marital intercourse during the *Shivah*.¹ Nor is it permitted to kiss and embrace² because such demonstrations are unseemly during the week of mourning.

SABBATH

Although the mourner does not observe public mourning at all on the Sabbath, this is nevertheless counted as a full day of *Shivah*.³ Support for this is found in the Palestinian Talmud⁴ in the commentary on the verse: 'The blessing of the Lord, it maketh rich, and toil addeth nothing thereto' (Prov. x: 22). Here the Talmud says that 'the blessing of the Lord maketh rich' refers to the blessing of the Sabbath, and the second part of the verse, 'And toil addeth nothing thereto,' infers that there is no public mourning on the Sabbath.

While mourners are forbidden to study, bath or cohabit on the Sabbath⁵ they do not have to sit on low stools and may change their clothes.⁶

SYNAGOGUE

In the Synagogue the mourner does not occupy his usual seat. This custom goes back to Talmudic times. Our Rabbis taught: 'When a *Chacham* (Sage) dies, his *Bet Hamidrash* (House of Study) is in vacation; when the *Av Bet Din* (Vice-President of the Supreme Court) dies, all the colleges in the city are in vacation and the people enter the Synagogues and change their usual places; those that usually sit in the north sit in the south and those that usually sit in the south sit in the north.⁷

¹ *Moed Katan* 15*b* and 21*a*; Y.D. 383.1; also during *Aninut* period Y.D. 341.5. (*Rema*).
² Y.D. 383.1 (*Rema*).
³ *Mishnah Moed Katan* 19*a*; Y.D. 400.1.
⁴ *Moed Katan* III.5.
⁵ Y.D. 400.1.
⁶ *Kitzur Shulchan Aruch* 195.6: 'Changing one's apparel for the Sabbath means putting on other weekly garments and not the usual Sabbath apparel'.
⁷ *Moed Katan* 22*b*.

Originally, this practice was followed only on the death of the Vice-President of the Court to indicate that his death had disrupted their lives. Nowadays, however, it is practised by all mourners.[1] A man mourning his parents should change his place for the whole year. His new place should be at least four cubits from his accustomed seat.

A mourner during the *Shivah* is not called up to the Torah even if he is the only Cohen or Levi in the congregation. If he is a Cohen or a Levi it is advisable for him to leave the Synagogue just before the Reading of the Law in order to avoid embarrassment both to himself and the congregation. If, however, he is inadvertently called up to the Torah he should not decline the *Mitzvah* and the usual *Mi-Sheberach* is made for him.

Rabbi Jacob b. Meir Tam[2] was regularly called up to the reading of the third portion of the *Sidra* every Sabbath. On the Sabbath of his bereavement he would not forgo his *Aliyah*. His argument was that any departure from the established practice would amount to a public demonstration of *Avelut*, which is forbidden on the Sabbath.[3]

A mourner who normally participates in the *Seudah Shelishit*[4] in the Synagogue may do so during the *Shivah*. He may ask for a Memorial Prayer to be said in memory of the deceased on Sabbath.[5] A grandfather who is sitting *Shivah*

---

[1] Cf. Y.D. 393.4. 'Those who adopt the practice when they are mourners not to change their places in the Synagogue on the Sabbath are correct in doing so.' The *Rema*, however, says: 'Some say that on the Sabbath he should also change his place, and this is the common practice, and one should not alter this custom.'

[2] *Rabbenu Tam* (1100–1171) a French *Tosaphist* and a grandson of Rashi.

[3] Y.D. 400.1.

[4] The 'Third Meal commences after *Minchah* and lasts until the end of the Sabbath. 'They shall recite the Afternoon Prayer,' says Maimonides, 'and commence the Third Meal and eat and drink until the expiry of the Sabbath.'

[5] *Orach Chayyim* 284.7 (*Rema*). On the other hand a number of rabbinic authorities do not permit it on Sabbath *Rosh Chodesh*, v. *Mishnah Berurah* ad. loc.

may attend his grandson's *Bar Mitzvah* Service, but he should not be called to the Reading of the Law.

FESTIVALS

There is no mourning on *Yom Tov*[1] so that if a death occurs during the Festival itself, mourning does not begin until the Festival is ended. A Cohen who is a mourner should not pronounce the priestly blessings on *Yom Tov*. It is preferable for him to leave the Synagogue before the beginning of the priestly benedictions.[2] If, however, only one other Cohen is present in the congregation, he may officiate during the twelve months period of mourning for his parents or during the *Sheloshim* for any other relative but not during the *Shivah*.

A mourner is forbidden, during the *Shivah*, to attend the Synagogue on the Eve of Passover to hear the *Siyyum*[3] which exempts the first-born from fasting that day.

Sukkot. One who becomes a mourner during the Feast of Tabernacles may be called up to the Torah on *Simchat Torah* (Rejoicing of the Law) but he may not be one of the Bridegrooms of the Law.[4] According to *Sephardi* custom[5] a mourner takes part in the *Hakkafot* (processional circuits).[6] *Ashkenazim* do not participate in the *Hakkafot* when mourning the loss of father or mother.[7]

It is customary for mourners to attend the Synagogue on the night of the 9th of *Av* to hear the Book of Lamentations (*Echah*) and in the daytime to recite the Prayers of Lamentations (*Kinot*)'[8] It is also permissible for them

[1] Maimonides, *Hilchot Avel* x: 13.
[2] *Orach Chayyim*, 128.43.
[3] Lit. 'Termination.' The completion of the study of a tractate of the Talmud. A special meal (*Seudah*) is held where the *Hadran* (concluding lecture) is delivered. See Greenwald, *op. cit.* p. 397.
[4] *Pitche Teshuvah* on Y.D. 399.1.
[5] Zimmels, *Ashkenazim and Sephardim*, p. 185.
[6] Around the Reading Desk while *Hoshanot* are chanted at the conclusion of the repetition of the *Musaph Amidah*.
[7] *Orach Chayyim* 661.2 (*Rema*).
[8] *Ibid*, 559.6.

to be called up to the Reading of the Law.[1]

The authorities are divided on the subject of mourning on *Purim*. Rabbi Joseph Caro[2] states that during the *Shivah* a mourner should observe all the laws of mourning. Rabbi Moses Isserles, on the other hand, quotes a number of authorities who maintained that 'outward' mourning is not observed on *Purim* or *Shushan Purim*.[3] The mourner is forbidden 'to witness any manner of festivity' but may put on his shoes and sit on a chair.[4] At night he can gather a *Minyan* to his house to hear the *Megillah*. If it is not possible to obtain a quorum he may go to the Synagogue.[5]

If *Purim* occurs at the termination of the Sabbath, the mourner should go to the Synagogue after the Third Meal while it is still Sabbath. A mourner during the *Shivah* period is permitted to send gifts to the needy and *Mishloach Manot* (gifts to friends and neighbours).[6] He should not, however, send anything of a joyous nature. It is, moreover, forbidden to send gifts during the entire twelve months[7] to one who is mourning for a parent.

The mourner is obliged to kindle lights during the festival of *Chanukah* and on the first night he recites the benediction, *Shehecheyanu* ('Who hast kept us alive').[8]

HEAD OF THE HOUSE

There are times when members of a family observing *Shivah* have to follow the lead of the head of the family. If a

[1] Greenwald, *op. cit.* p. 344.

[2] *Orach Chayyim* 696.4.

[3] *Ibid, Rema.* The 15th of *Adar* is known as *Shushan Purim* since in the capital, Shushan, the Jews had to defend themselves against their enemies on the 14th and celebrated the Festival a day later.

[4] *Kitzur Shulchan Aruch* 141.20.

[5] *Orach Chayyim* 696.4 (*Rema*).

[6] *Kitzur Shulchan Aruch* 142.7.

[7] *Ibid*, The *Magen Avraham* on *Orach Chayyim* (696.12) permits it. The *Taz*, on the other hand, forbids it.

[8] A benediction pronounced on occasions of importance. Greenwood, *op. cit.* p. 288, note 20. Some authorities do not permit an *Avel* to recite *Shehecheyanu* in public.

person comes from a nearby town (within a day's walking distance) and finds his relatives sitting *Shivah*, he should count the days of mourning with them. Even if he comes on the seventh day, he should still go according to their reckoning and consequently he will himself not need to observe *Shivah* again. This applies only where the head of the family (*Gedol habayit*)[1] is present and all other mourners follow the head of the family with regard to the *Shivah*.

If, however, the chief mourner comes from another town and finds members of the household sitting *Shivah*, he should begin to count for himself and in this case those who are already in mourning do not follow his lead.

SUICIDE

Although suicide is not classified in the *Mishnaic* Code as a criminal offence or a felony, it is regarded in Jewish teachings, if it is committed with full deliberation and by somebody of unquestionably sound mind, as a usurpation of the Divine prerogative, and a crime against both God and man. Despite all his sufferings Job did not even attempt to end his life: 'What shall we receive good at the hand of God,' he reasoned, 'and shall we not receive evil?' (Job II: 10).

In many cases, however, suicide is not an act of wanton self-destruction but a manifestation of intense despair. In the whole of the Bible there is mention of only a few people who took their lives and in each case the circumstances were exceptional. Each incident took place in a time of despair or when death by hostile hands was imminent. So it was with Ahithophel, Privy Councillor to David (II Sam. XVII: 23), Zimri (I Kings XVI: 18), Samson (Judges XVI: 28–30) and Saul (I Sam. XXXI: 4).

Josephus had strong views on suicide. 'Is it noble to destroy oneself?' he demanded with forceful rhetoric. 'Not so,

[1] 'One upon whom the people of the household depend and who are guided by him whether he is a brother or a young man.' Y.D. 375.2.

I reply, 'but most ignoble; in my opinion there could be no worse coward than the pilot who, for fear of a tempest, deliberately sinks his ship before the storm. No! Suicide is alike repugnant to the nature which all creatures share and an act of impiety towards God who created us.'[1]

Here, Josephus is in complete accord with Rabbinical teachings. The verse 'And surely your blood of your lives will I require' (Gen. IX: 5) is interpreted by the *Tanna* Rabbi Eleazar as: 'I will require your blood if shed by the hands of yourselves.'[2]

A suicide is called in Hebrew *Meabed Azmo Ladaat*[3], one who knowingly destroys himself. The Rabbis have never shared the opinion of Seneca (31 B.C.E.–30 C.E.) that the 'Eternal law that has assigned a single entrance to this life, has mercifully allowed many exits. Any death is preferable to servitude.'

The Jew is bidden to take great care of valuables, whether they are natural objects or human possessions. The special law of *Bal Tashchit*,[4] not to destroy,[5] is derived from the verse in Deuteronomy (XX: 19): 'When thou shalt besiege a city a long time, in making war against it to take it, thou shalt not destroy the trees thereof by wielding an axe against them; for thou mayest eat of them and thou shalt not cut them down; for is the tree of the field man that it should be besieged of thee?'

'He who in anger tears his clothes,' say the Rabbis,[6] 'and breaks crockery or throws away his money, is to be accounted as one who worships idols.' If this applies to inanimate objects, how much more serious it is for a man to extinguish his own life; for man created 'in the image of

---

[1] *The Jewish War*, III.344–362.
[2] *Baba Kamma* 91*b*.
[3] *Semachot* IV.
[4] Wanton destruction of property.
[5] *Kiddushin* 32.
[6] *Shabbat* 105*b*; *Avot d'Rabbi Nathan* III.1.

God' is deemed to be the centre of the creation, the glory of the world.

MARTYRDOM

It is a man's sacred duty to prolong and to preserve life by all the means within his power. 'Ye shall therefore keep My statutes, and Mine ordinances, which if man do, he shall live by them; I am the Lord' (Lev XVIII: 5). From this verse our Rabbis deduced that all negative commandments in the Torah, except those with regard to idolatry, immorality and murder, may be transgressed if life is in danger.[1] Yet the phenomenon of Jewish martyrdom, manifested in *Kiddush Hashem* (the Sanctification of God's Name) has few parallels in other cultures.

When the First Temple was destroyed, the priests leaped into the flames and died in their holy home.[2] Three years after the destruction of the Second Temple many of the heroes of Masada[3] killed themselves rather than submit to their cruel conquerors.[4] Jewish history is filled with accounts of similar sacrifices.

Anglo-Jewry, too, has notable acts of heroism to add to Israel's unending roll of martyrs. On the eve of the 'Great Sabbath' before Passover, March 16th, 1190, at the Clifford's Tower in York, England, Rabbi Yomtov of Joigny 'urged his co-religionists to anticipate their inevitable fate in heroic fashion. The number of victims was reported to exceed one hundred and fifty, besides those who met their death in the town.'[5] Tragedies such as these were enacted again and again during the Dark Ages, the Russian pogroms and the Nazi holocaust.

THE PROCEDURE FOR SUICIDE

The second chapter of the tractate *Semachot* and the Code

[1] *Sanhedrin 74a*; *Yerushalmi Sanhedrin* III.5; Y.D. 157.
[2] *Taanit 29a*.
[3] A stronghold west of the Dead Sea.
[4] Josephus, *War of the Jews* VII.1–7; IX.2.
[5] Cecil Roth, *History of the Jews in England*, p. 23.

Yoreh Deah[1] deals with the procedure to be adopted in the case of a suicide. 'One who commits suicide wilfully is not attended to at all; and one does not mourn for him and no lamentation is made for him, nor does one rend garments.' He is regarded as one who dies in a state of excommunication.[2] The Rabbis consider only a premeditated and deliberate act of self-destruction to be suicide; but when there is an act of aberration or sudden impulse, or where there is a doubt, a more lenient view is generally taken and the deceased is given 'the benefit of the doubt.' An instance is recorded in the Talmud. Threatened by his father with punishment, the young son of a citizen of Lydda ran away and killed himself. When the case was brought before Rabbi Tarphon (late 1st century C.E.), he decided that it was not suicide, saying that the boy was moved by fear of his father.[3]

According to the majority of rabbinic authorities, in most cases of suicide one may assume that the balance of his (or her) mind was disturbed. It was thought to be inconceivable that a person with a sound mind would commit such an abominable act. Many rabbinic authorities, therefore, permit surviving members of the family of a suicide to observe mourning and to recite *Kaddish* in the synagogue for the soul of the deceased. In this way they would be spared further humiliation and grief.[4]

If a minor commits suicide, it is regarded as if he had done the deed unintentionally.[5]

Mourning rites are not observed for apostates or for those who 'cast off the precepts from their necks and are not included among Israelites as regards the performance of the precepts.'[6] But a person who has been executed, even if he were an apostate, should be mourned.[7]

[1] *Semachot* 11; Y.D. 345.1.
[2] Y.D. 345.4.
[3] *Semachot* 11.4.
[4] *Pitche Teshuvah* on Y.D. 345.
[5] Y.D. 345.3.
[6] *Ibid*, s. 5 and *Kitzur Shulchan Aruch* 201.4; *Semachot* 11.10.
[7] *Kitzur Shulchan Aruch*, 201.5.

CHAPTER

VII

THE KADDISH

WHEN death visits a household, the whole house, indeed life itself, appears empty and the future bleak. At such a time, the son of the house rises in prayer and proclaims: 'Magnified and sanctified be His great Name in the world which He hath created according to His will. May He establish His kingdom during your life and during your days, and during the life of all the house of Israel, even speedily and at a near time, and say ye, Amen.'[1]

Thus, the *Kaddish* is a paean of praise, an affirmation of faith for all the world to hear. Three times a day, during the eleven-month period of the year of mourning, and on every *Yahrzeit*, a bereaved son affirms the greatness of God and honours his father's memory. His father is dead, but his spirit lives for ever. This is the fundamental meaning of the *Kaddish*, a prayer of almost mystical force, for it has bound successive generations together and it transcends the barriers of death.

Kaddish means sanctification, and the practice of saying *Kaddish* has become an integral part of Jewish life, since paradoxically it is connected with life and not with death.

The stress of modern living may have led to the non-observance of many religious rites, but it has not made less indestructible the *Kaddish* which is deeply ingrained in the minds and hearts of the people. It is a matter of honour with the majority of mourners not to miss a *Kaddish*, no matter

[1] A.P.B., p.80.

what hardship or inconvenience may be incurred in carrying out this act of filial duty and reverence. Jewish custom and usage may vary, but the familiar words of the *Kaddish* are heard wherever ten Jews join together for worship. The compulsive urge to say *Kaddish* is often a means of return to the Synagogue for many who have been totally or partially estranged from it. 'Help to make up a *minyan* for *Kaddish*' is a plea that few ignore.

HISTORY

Though verses of the *Kaddish* prayer are said to date from Patriarchal times,[1] the present text dates from the *Geonic* period.[2] The prayer had its origin in the school-house in the Holy Land, where it was recited by the teacher or preacher as a doxology at the conclusion of a Talmudic discourse. Later, the practice was continued in Babylon. The responses of the congregation were regarded as being of the utmost importance, and according to the *Targum* (Deut. VI: 4), Jacob made these responses. 'Joining loudly in unison in the congregational chorus of *Yehe Shemeh Rabbah*,' say the Rabbis, 'has the power of influencing the heavenly decree in one's favour, or of obtaining forgiveness.'[3] Similarly, Rabbi Jose b. Chalafta, a second-century teacher, affirms: 'Whenever the Israelites go into the Synagogues and school-houses and respond: "May His great name be blessed," the Holy One blessed be He, as it were, shakes his head and says, "Happy is the king who is thus praised in his house. Woe to the father who banished his children, and woe to the children who had to be banished from the table of their father." '[4] Again and again the Rabbis emphasise the importance of these verses. Rabbi Joshua ben Levi says that the evil decree is annulled for the man who makes the

[1] *Targum Yerushalmi* on Gen. XLIX: 2 and Deut. VI: 4.
[2] *Sopherim* XIX: 12 and *Siddur* of R. Amram *Gaon* (middle of the ninth century).
[3] *Shabbat* 119b.
[4] *Berachot* 3a.

responses with complete devotion, and Rabbi Chiyyah bar Abba, in the name of Rabbi Jochanan, goes even further. 'Even if he has a taint of idolatry, he is forgiven . . . and the gates of Paradise are opened to him.'[1]

Later the school-house doxology became part of the liturgy of the Synagogue. It is clear from the tractate *Sopherim* (of the *Geonic* period) that the Synagogue services at that time began with *Barechu* ('Bless ye the Lord Who is to be blessed') and the *Kaddish*, and concluded with the Reading of the Law and a second recital of the *Kaddish*.

MOURNER'S PRAYER

Perhaps the earliest reference to the *Kaddish* as a 'Mourner's Prayer' was made in the thirteenth century by Rabbi Isaac ben Moses of Vienna (ca. 1180–1260) in his book *Or Zarua*.[2] And it has been the practice ever since for both *Sephardi* and *Ashkenazi* mourners to recite the *Kaddish*, with minor textual variants. True, objections were occasionally made by leading authorities who were afraid that the *Kaddish* might become the centre of Judaic worship. 'They buoy themselves up with vain hope,' writes Rabbi Abraham b. Chiyya *ha-Nasi* (twelfth century) 'when they reckon that the actions and prayers of their sons would benefit them after death.'[3] The same sentiment was expressed by Rabbi Abraham Hurwitz in the sixteenth century. 'Let the son keep a particular precept given him by his father, and it would be of greater worth than the recitation of the *Kaddish*. The same is true also of daughters. For the *Kaddish* is not a prayer for the son that the father may be brought up from *Sheol* (the nether world of the grave), but a recognition of the parent's merit, since through its recital the child best vindicates the memory of his parent

---

[1] *Shabbat* 119b.
[2] *Or Zarua* II, p. 11b. 'It is our custom in the land of Canaan and it is the custom in the land of *Benei Rinus* that after the community recites *Ein Keloheinu*, the orphan recites *Kaddish*.'
[3] David de Sola Pool, *The Kaddish*, p. 105

by causing the congregation to respond to him with the praise *Amen, Yehe Shemeh Rabba.*'[1]

REDEEMING QUALITY

'Parental merit' (*Zechut Avot*) plays a great part in Jewish theology. 'For the merits of the fathers,' the Rabbis say, 'was Israel redeemed from Egypt.'[2] 'The Patriarchs, as well as other personages of the Bible, accomplished or came near to perfection by their faith and love, unselfishness and charity, observances and performances, studies and works —those ideals for which alone the world was worthy to be called into existence, and for which it deserves to exist. Thus they gathered treasures in heaven not for themselves but for others. By their works and charity their descendants experienced miracles and wonders in the course of their historical life. By their merits Israel escaped thousands of perils and dangers. For their sake Israel's immortality and eternity are assured.'[3]

Paradoxically, just as a father can intercede for his children so children can be of service to their parents, for the dead need to be forgiven and a man's son is his best advocate. There is an old Jewish belief that 'the son confers privileges on his father.'[4] Rabbi Akiva once saw in a vision the shadowy

---

[1] *Yesh Nochalin*, p. 35; David De Sola Pool, *op. cit.* p. 34. Elyakim b. Joseph the *Ravya* (d. 1150) writes: 'It is not generally accepted that through the recitation of the *Kaddish* the son brings his father and mother to Paradise, and that he who frequently repeats the *Kaddish* atones by that action for the sins of his parents and helps them to enter into the future world. For there is no foundation for the view that the *Kaddish* is for the mourners. There is no basis for it in either the Jerusalem or the Babylonian Talmud or in the *Tosephta*. The only source is the legend of Rabbi Akiva, and we do not base laws upon legends.' A. Berliner, *Randbemerkungen*, Vol. I, p. 69, also A. Z. Idelsohn, *Jewish Liturgy and its Development*, p. 87.

[2] Exodus *Rabbah* xv.5.

[3] A. Marmorstein, *The Doctrine of Merit in Old Rabbinical Literature*, pp. 155–6.

[4] *Sanhedrin* 104a.

figure of a man carrying a load of wood upon his shoulders. 'What aileth thee?' asked the Rabbi. 'I am one of those forlorn souls condemned for his sins to the agony of hell-fire,' replied the shadow. 'And there is no hope for you?' enquired the Rabbi further in great compassion. 'If my little son, who was a mere infant when I died, could be taught to recite the *Kaddish*, then and only then would I be absolved.' The Rabbi took the boy under his care and taught him to lisp the *Kaddish*. He was then assured that the father had been released from *Gehenna*.[1]

By piety and devotion men can intercede successfully for those who have sinned during their lifetime. For example, when David heard of Absalom's death, he uttered the cry, 'My son, Absalom,' eight times and with each heart-rending cry, say the Rabbis, raised his son up by stages out of his misery.[2] The righteousness of a living child favourably affects the destiny of a dead parent. 'The old Jewish doctrine of the merit of the fathers has a counterpart—the idea that the righteousness of the living child favourably affects the fate of the dead father. This might be called the doctrine of the 'merit of the children.' In this way the living and the dead hold converse. The real message of the dead is their virtue. The response of the living is again their virtue. Thus is a bridge built over the chasm of the tomb. Thus do the hearts of fathers and children beat in eternal unison.'[3]

SUBMISSION TO THE WILL OF GOD

The *Kaddish* further declares man's submission to the will of God. Although there is no reference to death in the *Kaddish*, its clear implication is, 'His will, not ours, be done.' When a man's grief is almost unbearable and his heart is full of sorrow, the *Kaddish* prayer, 'Magnified and hallowed

[1] Marmorstein, *op. cit.* p. 156; Kallah (ed. Coronel), pp. 4*b*, 19*b*. In *Psalm Eliyahu Zutta* II (ed. Friedmann, p. 22) the story is told in the name of Rabban Jochanan ben Zakkai.
[2] *Sotah* 10*b*.
[3] I. Abrahams, quoted in *A Book of Jewish Thoughts*, p. 198.

be His great name,' is a wonderful way for him proudly and publicly, to proclaim his unshakable faith that 'whatever the Merciful One does, it is for good.'[1]

The *Kaddish* 'possesses wonderful power. Truly, if there is any bond strong and indissoluble enough to chain heaven to earth, it is this prayer. It keeps the living together, and forms the bridge to the mysterious realm of the dead. One might almost say that this prayer is the watchman and the guardian of the people by whom alone it is uttered; therein lies the warrant of its continuance. Can a people disappear and be annihilated so long as a child remembers its parents? It may sound strange: in the midst of the wildest dissipation has this prayer recalled to his better self many a dissolute character, so that he has bethought himself and for a time at least purified himself by honouring the memory of his parents.

Because this prayer is a resurrection in the spirit of the perishable in man, because it does not acknowledge death, because it permits the blossom which, withered, has fallen from the tree of mankind to flower and develop again in the human heart, therefore it possesses sanctifying power. To know that when thou diest, the earth falling on thy head will not cover thee entirely; to know that there remain behind those who, wherever they may be on this wide earth, whether they may be poor or rich, will send this prayer after thee; to know that thou leavest them no house, no estate, no field by which they must remember thee, and that yet they will cherish thy memory as their dearest inheritance—what more satisfying knowledge canst thou ever hope for? And such is the knowledge bequeathed to us all by the *Kaddish*.'[2]

RESURRECTION AND KADDISH

Judaism stresses the 'immortality of the soul' and the 'revival of the dead.' True, the *Kaddish* makes no reference

[1] *Berachot*, 60b.
[2] Leopold Kompert (1822–1886) quoted in *A Book of Jewish Thoughts*, pp. 199–200.

to the Resurrection, but it does refer (more markedly so in the *Sephardic* version) to the Messianic vision.[1] The resurrection is closely interwoven with the Coming of the Messiah and the universal acknowledgment of the Unity of God. In the *Kaddish*, the mourner reaffirms his conviction in the hereafter. 'The dust returneth to the earth as it was; but the spirit returneth unto God who gave it.' (Ecc. XII: 7).

THE LANGUAGE

Apart from the closing verse, 'He Who maketh peace in His high places, may He make peace for us and for all Israel, and say ye Amen,' the original language of the *Kaddish* was Aramaic. For nearly a thousand years (from the time of Ezra to well after the end of the Talmudic period) Aramaic was the vernacular of the Jewish masses in Babylon and Palestine. Several passages and sections of the Bible[2] were written in Aramaic; as were the *Targumim*, much of the Palestinian Talmud (Talmud *Yerushalmi*), the Babylonian Talmud (Talmud *Bavli*), *Midrashim*, the *Masorah*, the *Geonic* writings, liturgical works and Cabbalistic literature. Though the sacred liturgy is for most part in *Lashon Ha-Kodesh* (the Holy tongue), the Hebrew Prayer Book still retains a number of Aramaic prayers[3] including the *Kaddish*.[4]

---

[1] *Veyatzmach Purkonay Vikoraiv Meshichai*, 'May He bring forth his salvation and hasten the coming of his anointed one.' In the *Siddur Ari* (Rabbi Isaac Luria) the text reads *Keitz Meshichai*, 'the end of the appointed time.'

[2] Gen. XXXI: 47; Ezra IV: 23—v: 5; VI: 13–18; Daniel II: 4;VII: 8.

[3] A.P.B., pp. 76–78; *Yekum Purkan*, in the Sabbath morning service, pp. 201–203; the introductory sentences of the Passover *Haggadah* and *Piyyutim* for penitential days.

[4] The Zohar (*Terumah* 129b) gives an additional reason: 'The *Kaddish* breaks down iron walls and weighty seals and all the shells and defences of Evil. By its merits the glory of the Holy One, Blessed be He, is more greatly exalted than through any other prayer, because it causes the power of the "other side" to wane and its empire to decline. Therefore, it must be said in Aramaic, which is the language of the "other side." ' Cf. *The Kaddish* by Marvin Luban, N.Y., 1962, p. 20.

DURATION

At first the *Kaddish* was recited during the whole twelve months of mourning.[1] 'The memory of the dead,' says the Talmud[2], 'begins to grow dim in the heart when twelve months have passed away.' But as twelve months were regarded as the maximum period of punishment accorded to the wicked in *Gehenna*,[3] Rabbi Moses b. Israel Isserles (ca. 1525–1572), of Cracow, limited the recital of the *Kaddish* to eleven months[4] (even in a leap year), for it would be unfilial for a man to assume that his parent had deserved the maximum penalty. Thus the *Kaddish* is recited for eleven months less one day.

Originally a son recited the *Kaddish* in memory of parents only. Gradually the practice was extended and other relatives also joined in this prayer. Nowadays, *Kaddish* is recited for close relatives: for a wife, sister, brother, son, daughter when they have no son of their own to recite the *Kaddish*.[5] Grandchildren may say *Kaddish* for their grandparents, and pupils for their teachers. If the mourner's parents are living, he should not recite *Kaddish* for another relative. 'It is the adopted usage to recite *Kaddish* for one's mother although the father is still living and the latter has no right to prevent his son from reciting *Kaddish* for his mother.'[6]

When there are no children or relatives, a stranger, provided that he is a pious man, may be deputed to recite *Kaddish* for the deceased.[7] A man should not undertake to recite *Kaddish* for two people at the same time.

It is the general view of Rabbinic authorities that

[1] *Kol Bo* cxvi.
[2] *Berachot* 58b.
[3] *Rosh Hashanah* 17a; *Shabbat* 33b.
[4] Y.D. 376.4 (*Rema*).
[5] Greenwald, *op. cit.* p. 375.
[6] Y.D. 376.4 (*Rema*).
[7] Greenwald, *op. cit.* p. 376 in the name of the *Noda Biyehudah*, *Orach Chayyim* 8.

daughters, even in the absence of sons, do not recite *Kaddish* in the Synagogue.[1] If, however, the daughter wishes to honour her departed father she should listen attentively to the recitation of the *Kaddish* and respond 'Amen' with devotion, in which case it is regarded as if she herself had said *Kaddish* and fulfilled the precept.

It is worth noting that several Rabbinic authorities saw no objection to daughters saying the *Kaddish* prayer. For example, the famous Chassidic woman—Channah Rachel (1815–1892), the Maid of Ludomir, an only daughter—recited *Kaddish* in memory of her father, Monesh Werbermacher.

CONGREGATIONAL PRAYER

The *Kaddish* can only be recited if there is a *minyan*.[2] This conforms with the liturgical maxim in the Talmud:[3] 'Words of holiness and sanctification need a religious quorum of ten males for their recitation.' Whoever recites *Kaddish* must do this standing. In some communities it is general practice for the congregation also to stand; in Eastern Europe the congregation remained seated.

Worshippers must maintain strictest decorum during the *Kaddish*. According to Rabbi Chezekiah de Silva (d. 1698), author of *Pri-Chadash*, it is even forbidden to mediate upon the words of the Torah during this prayer, for attention must be paid to every single word of the *Kaddish* and its responses. The *Zohar* states that 'whosoever talks in the Synagogue while the congregation is occupied in the praise of God, shows that he has no portion in the God of Israel

[1] *Beer Hetev, Orach Chayyim* 132.

[2] Zohar II, 129b, 'The *Shechinah* unites herself with the Holy tongue and all sanctifications with which the *Shechinah* is connected can be uttered only in the presence of at least ten persons.' Cf. however, *Sopherim* x: 7.

[3] *Berachot* 21b. It is derived from the verse: 'I shall be sanctified in the midst of the children of Israel' (Lev. xxii: 32).

and his sin is very grievous'. It is also strictly forbidden to pass in front of a man reciting the *Kaddish*.

RECITATION OF KADDISH

The custom today is for every mourner to recite *Kaddish*. Among the *Sephardim* the *Minhag* is for mourners to recite the *Kaddish* in unison.

The mourner's *Kaddish* is recited at certain points in the service: after the *Alenu* ('It is our duty')[1] at the end of the statutory Services; after the Daily Psalm;[2] after the Hymn of Glory (*Anim Zemirot*)[3] and after Psalm xxx in the Morning Service.[4]

At the end of the *Kaddish*, as at the end of the *Amidah*, the worshipper takes three steps backwards as would a person withdrawing from the presence of a king.

During the Ten Days of Penitence, as a reminder that God reigns supreme above all creatures, the word *Leela* ('though He be high above') is added, and the two words *Min Kol* are contracted into one word *Mikol*. The sentence from *Yehe Shemeh Rabba* to *Olmaya* contains 28 letters equalling the numerical value of the word *Koah* (Power) and mystics point out that both by their meaning and by the number of letters that sentence represents our acknowledgment of the power of God, and by reciting this declaration Israel clothes itself with strength.

LAWS OF PRECEDENCE

Leading Rabbinical authorities in the past such as Rabbi Shabbethai ben Meir ha-Cohen (*Shach*) and Rabbi David ben Samuel ha-Levi (*Taz*)[5] set down a rigid order of precedence. A resident takes precedence over a stranger. If

---

[1] A.P.B., p. 79, p. 114, p. 132, p. 165, p. 222.
[2] A.P.B., pp. 84–89; *Orach Chayyim* 132.2 (*Rema*).
[3] A.P.B., pp. 81–84.
[4] *Ibid*, p. 17.
[5] Y.D. 376.

several *Yahrzeit* mourners are present, the *Kaddishim* are divided among them to the exclusion of others. A mourner who is sitting *Shivah* takes precedence over a stranger as well as over one observing a *Yahrzeit*. If there were more *Yahrzeit* mourners than there were *Kaddishim* in the service, lots were drawn. As these rules frequently lead to contention, modern Ashkenazi practice is that all mourners recite the *Kaddish*.

THE RABBINICAL KADDISH

Kaddish De-Rabbanan[1] (Scholar's *Kaddish*) was so named because it was recited upon the completion of a division of the *Mishnah* or of a tractate of the Talmud or after a discourse; and the reciter should, if possible, take part in the study course.

It is also recited after the *Beraita*[2] (of Rabbi Ishmael) in the Morning Service,[3] after the quotation from the tractate *Berachot* 'Rabbi Eleazar said in the name of Rabbi Chaninah' at the conclusion of *Bameh Madlikin* on Friday night[4], and at the conclusion of the Sabbath *Musaph* Service if the Talmudic reading *Pitum Haketoret* is recited.[5]

BURIAL KADDISH

Apart from the 'Half-*Kaddish*' (*Chatzi Kaddish*) which marks the end of certain sections of the Service, the 'full *Kaddish*' (*Kaddish Shalem*), the mourner's *Kaddish* (*Kaddish Yatom*), the Rabbinical *Kaddish*[6] (*Kaddish Derabbanan*), there is also the *Kaddish leithadata* (*Kaddish* of Renewal)[7] which is recited by sons at the interment of parents. It is omitted on

[1] A.P.B., p. 15.
[2] Lit. outside. A teaching of the *Tannaim* that has been excluded from the *Mishnah*.
[3] A.P.B., p. 15.
[4] *Mishnah Shabbat* 11. A.P.B., pp. 161–162.
[5] *Keritot* 6a. A.P.B., pp. 219–20.
[6] A.P.B., p. 15.
[7] *Ibid*, p. 428.

those days when *Tachanun*[1] is not said. The theme of the Burial *Kaddish* is, 'God will revive the dead and raise them up into life eternal. He will rebuild the City of Jerusalem and establish His Temple in the midst thereof.'

This prayer was also originally used as a doxology by the scholars after a homiletical discourse in rabbinical colleges. Today, however, the Burial *Kaddish* is recited by all mourners at funerals. It may be truly said that the *Kaddish* has become a link between the generations, between man and God, and between man and man.

[1] *Ibid*, pp. 60–68.

CHAPTER

VIII

THE PERIOD OF MOURNING

JUDAISM disagrees with the philosophy of life of the eminent humanist, Dr Albert Schweitzer, who said 'Unrest, disappointment and pain are our lot . . . All life is suffering.' The Jew believes that his religion gives him guidance at all times; it upholds him in times of gladness and of sorrow; in moments of exaltation and of deep despair. For every aspect of life Judaism has its counsel. In bereavement, when man's mind and emotions are so powerfully challenged, Judaism teaches how to give expression to one's sense of loss, how to regain one's composure, one's zest, indeed inspiration for one's own life and that of future generations.

The Rabbis discourage excessive mourning; 'Weep ye not for the dead,' says Jeremiah, 'neither bemoan him' (Jer. XXII: 10), and this has been interpreted by the Sages as 'weep not in excess, nor bemoan too much.' This concept should, according to the Talmud, be carried out in the following way: 'Three days are set aside for weeping and seven days for lamentation and thirty days to refrain from cutting the hair and donning pressed clothes; thereafter, the Holy One Blessed be He, says: "Ye are not more compassionate towards him (the departed) than I ".'[1]

During the thirty days (the *Sheloshim*) the change from the sadness of bereavement to normal life gradually takes place. There are several references in the Torah to this thirty-day period of mourning. For instance, 'The whole House of Israel wept for Aaron for thirty days' (Num. XX:

[1] *Moed Katan* 27b.

29), and for Moses too, the children of Israel wept 'for thirty days, so that the days of weeping for Moses were ended' (Deut. xxxiv: 8). Similarly in *Mishnaic* times, Rabbi Judah Hanasi, before he died, gave instructions that the 'assembly for study should be reconstituted after the lapse of thirty days from the day of his death.'[1]

The relatives for whom the period of *Sheloshim* is observed are: father, mother, husband, wife, brother, sister, son and daughter.[2]

The period of the *Sheloshim* starts on the day of the funeral and ends on the morning of the thirtieth day. If this should fall on a Sabbath, a mourner may wear his Sabbath clothes and bathe in warm water before the Sabbath but he must not cut his hair on the Friday before.[3]

TIMELY OR DISTANT NEWS

If a mourner learns of the death of a relative within thirty days the news is regarded as 'timely' (*Shemuah Kerovah*).[4]

The mourner must then sit *Shivah*, rend his clothes and count the period of *Sheloshim* from the day of the report. If, however, he receives news of a death more than thirty days after it has taken place, the news is regarded as 'delayed' or 'distant' (*Shemuah Rechokah*) and mourning need only be observed for one hour.

In the latter event he need only remove his shoes and sit on a low stool. He is not required to tear his clothes unless the death is that of a parent.[5] The remainder of the twelve

---

[1] *Ketubot* 103*b*.

[2] It is interesting to note that the Hebrew word *Avel* has been used as a mnemonic to remind people where their duty lay. For *Aleph*, the first letter can stand for *Ish* (man), *Ishah* (woman), *Av* (father), *Em* (mother), *Ach* (brother), or *Achot* (sister); while *Bet*, the second letter, stands for *Ben* (son) or *Bat* (daughter). In addition, *Lamed*, the third letter, is the sign for thirty (Sheloshim) (see Abraham Lewysohn, *Sepher Mekore Minhagim Hanehugim Bivnei Yisrael*, Berlin, 1846, p. 136).

[3] *Kitzur Shulchan Aruch*, 216.2.

[4] Y.D. 402.

[5] Y.D. 340.18.

months of mourning must be observed by commencing counting from the day of death.

One who has received 'timely' news on the Sabbath should count the Sabbath as one day and at the termination of the Sabbath he should rend his garments and observe six days of mourning thereafter.[1]

During the *Sheloshim*, a mourner must not take part in any festivity or attend any place of entertainment whether on the Sabbath, a Festival or a weekday. If he mourns a parent, this period of abstinence should continue for the full twelve months.[2] He should not listen to instrumental music or play any musical instruments himself during the whole period of mourning.

Some authorities differentiate between a 'feast,' which is of a purely secular or social nature, and a *Seudat Mitzvah*, a meal which is primarily of a religious significance.[3] 'A mourner is forbidden to join in the circumcision feast, or in the feast to celebrate the redemption of the first-born, or on the occasion of the conclusion of a tractate of the *Mishnah* or Talmud, and more especially a wedding feast, during the thirty days of his mourning for one's relatives and during the year for one's parents.'[4]

It is permissible for the mourner after the seven days of mourning to enter the Synagogue where they recite the bethrothal and wedding benedictions and where there is no joyous entertainment.[5] Some authorities prohibit this until after the *Sheloshim* and, 'this seems to me,' writes Rabbi Moses Isserles, 'to be the correct view.'[6]

A mourner for a parent may act as *Unterführer*[7] provided it is after the period of *Sheloshim*. A mourner for other near-

[1] Y.D. 402.7.
[2] Y.D. 391.2.
[3] Y.D. 391.2.
[4] *Kitzur Shulchan Aruch* 212.1.
[5] Y.D. 391.3.
[6] Y.D. 391.3.
[7] or *Unterfirer* (Yiddish): a close relative who conducts the bride or groom under the wedding canopy.

of-kin is permitted to be an *Unterführer* even during the *Sheloshim*.[1] If a mourner for a parent gives in marriage an orphan he may attend the wedding ceremony and participate in the festivities.[2] Some authorities permit a mourner to eat at a wedding banquet or a circumcision 'with those who wait upon the guests, provided it is not in a place of joyous entertainment.'[3]

A Rabbi or a Reader in mourning over a parent is permitted by some authorities to attend a wedding celebration even within the *Sheloshim*, if it is a question of losing a livelihood.[4] For example, a musician is permitted to play music during the twelve months of mourning for a parent or within the *Sheloshim* for other relatives.[5] Parents who are in mourning may participate in the wedding celebration of their son or daughter.

NO SHELOSHIM

If burial takes place before a Festival and the mourner observes the mourning rites even for one hour prior to the Festival, the *Yom Tov* annuls the entire *Shivah* period.[6] If the *Shivah* is completed prior to the Festival, then the incoming Festival cancels the *Sheloshim* period in its entirety.[7] The *Sheloshim* are not suspended when mourning goes for one's father or mother. The mourner is not allowed to 'cut his hair until he is reproved by his friends.'

If the mourner observes the *Shivah* prior to the commencement of the New Year, the *Sheloshim* come to an end with the advent of the Day of Atonement. Similarly, if the *Shivah* terminates during the Ten Days of Penitence, the *Sheloshim*

---

[1] Y.D. 391.3.

[2] *Ibid.*

[3] Y.D. 391.3 (*Rema*).

[4] Provided there is no musical entertainment there. The *Minchat Eleazer*, however, forbids it.

[5] *Shulchan Aruch Yoreh Deah*, tran. by Chaim N. Denburg, p. 330, note 38.

[6] Y.D. 399.1.

[7] *Ibid.*

come to an end with the commencement of the Day of Atonement.[1]

If the mourner observes *Shivah* even for a short time prior to the Festival of Passover it is regarded as if he had observed seven days of *Shivah*, and with the 'eight days' of Passover added we have fifteen days. The *Sheloshim* are thus terminated fifteen days after Passover.[2] Similarly, if he has observed one hour of *Shivah* prior to the Festival of Pentecost, only fifteen days are observed after the festival.

If he has observed *Shivah* prior to the Festival of Tabernacles, he need only observe eight days after the Festival to complete the period of *Sheloshim*.[3] If, however, the funeral takes place on *Chol Hamoed*, the *Shivah* is observed at the termination of the Festival and the *Sheloshim* follows suit.[4] The last day of the Festival counts as one of the days of the *Shivah* and *Sheloshim*.[5]

HAIRCUT

The mourner for other relatives should not cut his hair or beard during the *Sheloshim*. However, if he is mourning for his father or his mother, he should let his hair grow until his friends remark on its untidiness. 'The common practice,' says Rabbi Moses Isserles, 'is to wait three months. And in these localities it is the adopted practice not to cut one's hair when in mourning for a father or mother, during the entire twelve months of mourning, unless the need is great, e.g. if his hair is too heavy upon him or he goes among Gentiles and appears repulsive to them with his hair, in which case he is permitted to cut his hair.'[6]

Rabbi Moses Schreiber (1763–1839), the *Chatam Sopher*, regarded as the foremost Rabbinical authority of his time, reports that his teachers once permitted an individual, even during the seven days of mourning for his father, to cut his hair, wash and put on pressed garments in order to see a royal personage with whom he had an appointment, the

[1] *Ibid*, s. 9.   [2] *Moed Katan* 24b; Y.D. 399.7.
[3] *Ibid*, s. 11.   [4] *Ibid*, s. 2.
[5] *Ibid*.   [6] Y.D. 390.4 (*Rema*).

postponement of which would have entailed great loss to the individual.[1]

Just as it is forbidden to cut hair during the entire thirty days of mourning so also is it forbidden to cut one's nails with scissors.[2] Combing the hair is allowed even during the first seven days of mourning.[3]

MOURNING CLOTHES

It used to be the custom for mourners to wear black throughout the *Sheloshim* since black was regarded as the symbol of death. The *Aggadah* quotes Moses as saying: 'Joshua, put on black clothes after my death.' Simeon the Just (end of the fourth century B.C.E.) predicted his approaching death. When he was asked how he knew this, he replied: 'On every Day of Atonement an old man, dressed in white . . . would join me entering the Holy of Holies . . . But today I was joined by an old man dressed in black.'[4]

Jews would normally wear dark clothes, as Israel Abrahams writes,[5] 'The Jews of all countries wore black; in Spain, Germany and Italy the phenomenon was equally marked. Black being the colour of grief the Jews—"mourners of Zion" as they were called—were no doubt strengthened in their predilection for black on the score of modesty, by its applicability to their persecuted state.'

In mourning for Jerusalem, the Talmud records[6] that the Jews wore black shoes. In the Middle Ages there was a sect of Jews who always deliberately wore black as a sign of perpetual mourning.[7]

---

[1] Responsa on *Orach Chayyim* (Pressburg, 1855) No. 158, p. 61.
[2] Y.D. 390.7.
[3] *Ibid*, 390.5.
[4] *Yoma* 39b.
[5] *Jewish Life in the Middle Ages*, p. 315.
[6] *Baba Kamma* 59b. When Eliezer Zeera was asked: What grounds have you for wearing black shoes? He said to them 'I am mourning for Jerusalem.'
[7] Benjamin of Tudelo (ed. Asher) 1, p. 113 and Abrahams, *op. cit.* p. 315, note 4.

In London, until the second half of the nineteenth century, all the principal mourners attending a funeral were given black 'mourners' cloaks' which were worn throughout the week of the *Shivah*.[1] In Amsterdam it was the custom among the *Sephardim* for mourners who attended the Synagogue on Sabbath afternoon to be dressed in black.

Nowadays, however, Orthodox Jews do not wear black for mourning and the wearing of a black armband is regarded as *Chukkat Hagoy*.

A woman in mourning who has given birth to a child and who wishes to go to the Synagogue on a Sabbath may wear her best garments and jewellery.

MOURNING AND MARRIAGE LAWS

'The mourner is forbidden to take a wife during the entire thirty days of mourning, even without making a wedding feast, but after the *Sheloshim* he is permitted, even if he is mourning for his father or mother, to marry and to make a wedding feast.'[2] He is permitted to betroth a wife prior to the termination of the *Sheloshim*. Many Rabbinic authorities, however, assert that 'betrothal is forbidden during the entire thirty days of mourning' and this is the view which Rabbi Moses Isserles follows.[3]

A man whose wife has died should wait until at least three Festivals have elapsed before he remarries.[4] In this connection the New Year, the Day of Atonement and *Shemini Atzeret* (The Feast of the Eighth Day) are not regarded as Festivals.[5] In exceptional cases such as that of a widower with very young children and with no one to look after them, the marriage may be allowed earlier.

The period of waiting serves a double purpose: a man ought not to forget his first wife too quickly; and he will better appreciate his new wife after a period of loneliness.

[1] Cecil Roth, *History of the Great Synagogue*, p. 104.
[2] Y.D. 392.1.
[3] *Ibid.*
[4] *Moed Katan* 23a.
[5] Y.D. 392.2.

A widow is forbidden to re-marry until ninety days have elapsed after the death of her husband.

If one of the immediate relatives of the bride or bridegroom died, the wedding should be deferred until after the *Shivah*.[1]

THE YEAR OF MOURNING

For the twelve-month period of mourning various reasons are given. According to the *Zohar*,[2] the soul clings to the body for twelve months. The Talmud, on the other hand, says: 'For twelve months the body is in existence and the soul ascends and descends; after twelve months the body ceases to exist and the soul ascends but descends no more.'[3] It was furthermore believed that purification in after life takes place in the first twelve months and that after a year the memory wanes.

VISITING THE CEMETERY

There is no uniform custom with regard to visiting the grave during the first year of mourning. Some people purposely refrain from visiting it during this year. Others visit the cemetery frequently and some do so on the last day of the *Shivah*. In Spain it was customary to visit the grave during the first week of mourning.[4]

The popular idea that the grave must not be visited during the first twelve months after death is not to be found in Jewish teachings. Indeed it was believed that the dead take an interest in the living and intercede for them[5] and visits for the purpose of beseeching such intercessions were not discouraged. Jacob buried Rachel near Ephrath at Bet-Lechem (Gen. xxxv: 19) so that she might pray for her children as they passed by her grave on their way to the Babylonian exile. 'Rachel weeping for her children, she

---

[1] *Kitzur Shulchan Aruch* 213.3.
[2] *Vayyechi* 225a.
[3] *Shabbat* 152b.
[4] Zimmels, *Ashkenazim and Sephardim*, p. 185.
[5] *Taanit* 16a; *Sotah* 34b.

refuseth to be comforted for her children because they are not' (Jer. xxxi: 15). And Caleb, one of the twelve spies[1] who went to explore the land of Canaan, is reported to have gone to the graves of the Patriarchs and prayed: 'My fathers, pray on my behalf that I may be delivered from the plans of the spies.'[2]

It has always been regarded as a *Mitzvah* to visit the graves of saintly people and beseech their aid—a common practice among the *Tannaim* and *Amoraim*. The Talmud records that 'it is the custom of the people to take earth from the grave of the Babylonian *Amora* Rav[3] and apply it as a remedy on the first day of an attack of fever.[4] During the Fast Days they would go to the cemetery 'in order that the departed ones should pray for mercy on our behalf.'[5]

However, visiting the grave too often was discouraged as it might lead to attempts to communicate with the dead by spiritualistic means and this was forbidden in the Torah. 'There shall not be found among you . . . a charmer or one that consulteth a ghost or a familiar spirit or a necromancer' (Deut. xviii: 10-12). Necromancy was classified with idolatry and magic, and 'those that dig up the dead' and 'those who predict by means of the bones of the dead' have no place in Judaism. Sleeping in cemeteries was considered one of the signs of insanity.[6] The Talmud enumerates five things which 'cause the man who does them to foreit his life and his blood is upon his own head'. One of these is sleeping in a cemetery in order to obtain an 'unclean spirit.'[7]

It is traditional to visit the cemetery on the 9th of *Av*,[8] during the month of *Elul*,[9] during the Ten Days of Penitence and on the eve of *Rosh Hashanah* and particularly on the eve

---

[1] Numbers XIII.
[2] *Sotah* 34*b*.
[3] *Abba Areka* 160–247.
[4] *Sanhedrin* 47*b*.
[5] *Taanit* 16*a*.
[6] *Hagigah* 3*b*.
[7] *Niddah* 17*a* and *Sanhedrin* 65*b*.
[8] *Orach Chayyim* 559.10 (*Rema*).
[9] *Ibid*, 581.4 (*Rema*).

of *Yom Kippur*[1] and on a parent's *Yahrzeit* or on the day
before.[2] Special prayers (*Techinot*) in books known as *Maane
Loshon* (The Answer of the Tongue)[3] were recited. Rabbi
Judah the Pious (d. 1217), however, prohibited visits to a
grave twice in one day.[4]

It is a common practice among those who accept the
mystical way of life to 'invite' dead parents to take part at
a *Simchah*; for the mystics believe that even in the world of
eternity the souls of the departed derive pleasure on hearing
good news.

Those orthodox Jewish authorities who do not approve
of decorating graves with flowers do so because in their
view this constitutes *Chukat Hagoy*.

ADDITIONAL CUSTOMS

A mourner must not officiate as a Reader on Sabbath,
Festivals,[5] New Moon, *Purim* or on the first night of
Chanukah during the entire year unless there be no other
Reader. However, if prior to his having become a mourner
he had been accustomed to act as Reader on the Sabbaths
and Festivals, he may also act as such during the mourning
period.[6] A professional Reader may conduct services in the
Synagogue during the period of mourning.

A mourner should not light the *Chanukah* lights in the
Synagogue on the first night as he is required to say the
benediction *Shehecheyanu* ('who kept us in life') but he may
recite the blessing in his own home.

A mourner even in the first seven days of mourning is
obliged to send gifts to the needy on *Purim*. Gifts, however,
are not sent to a mourner for the entire twelve months of
mourning.

[1] *Ibid*, 605 (*Rema*).
[2] See below.
[3] From the sentence in Proverbs XVI: 1 'The preparations of the
heart are man's but the answer of the tongue is from the Lord.'
[4] *Sepher Ha-Chassidim*, ed. Wistinetzki, p. 271.
[5] *Kitzur Shulchan Aruch* 26.14, 210.5.
[6] *Ibid*.

A minor need not observe any of the laws of mourning.

The clothing of a deceased person who did not die of a contagious disease should not be destroyed. They should be given to the poor.

THE COHEN AND MOURNING RITES

A *Cohen* is forbidden to enter a house where there is a corpse. He is even forbidden to enter a house where a person is dying as death may occur at any moment and thus cause his defilement. Nor may he go within four cubits[1] of a grave.[2] However, these prohibitions do not apply when he has lost a father, mother, son, daughter, wife, brother or unmarried sister from his father's side.[3] The reason for these prohibitions is that a high standard of purity was demanded of the priests, 'the emissaries not of the people but of God.'

Those who have not visited the burial ground for thirty days say the following: 'Blessed be the Lord our God, King of the universe, who formed you in judgment, who nourished and sustained you in judgment, who brought death on you in judgment, who knoweth the number of you in judgment, and will hereafter restore you to life in judgment. Blessed art thou, O Lord who quickenest the dead.

Thou, O Lord, art mighty for ever, thou revivest the dead, thou art mighty to save.

'Thou sustainest the living with lovingkindness, revivest the dead with great mercy, supportest the falling, healest the sick, loosest the bound, and keepest thy faith to them that sleep in the dust. Who is like unto thee, Lord of mighty acts and who resembleth thee, O King, who causeth death and revivest and causeth salvation to spring forth? Yea, faithful art thou to revive the dead.'[4]

[1] Six feet.
[2] Y.D. 371.5.
[3] Lev. XXI: 1 'He shall not defile himself for the dead among his people.' See *Sifra* and Y.D. 374.4.
[4] A.P.B. pp. 426–7; *Berachot* 58*b*.

CHAPTER

IX

THE YAHRZEIT
(Anniversary of a Death)

LIKE the *Kaddish*, the *Yahrzeit* is a powerful magnet, drawing a man back to the Synagogue and back to his people with regular and incessant rhythm. Even those whose Synagogue affiliations are slender indeed, make new contact on this memory-hallowed day. Even in small communities, where there is no regular *minyan* and where the House of Prayer is closed the entire week, even there the doors of the Synagogue are opened and arrangements are made for a service to take place when a Jew has a *Yahrzeit* to observe. For the observance of the *Yahrzeit* is one of the honours that a man can pay his departed parents and it is a duty that his heart and mind and conscience bid him pay with scrupulous care. As the strains of the *Yahrzeit Kaddish* reverberate through the soul they re-awaken with indescribable poignancy the faded memories of past years.

'And it was a custom in Israel, that the daughters of Israel went yearly to lament the daughter of Jephthah, the Gileadite, four days in a year' (Judges xi: 40). This is the first scriptural reference to *Yahrzeit*, which was widely observed in Talmudic times,[1] when many people fasted on the anniversary of a parent's death. The traditional date of the death of Moses is observed on the 7th Adar. Natronai Gaon, head of the academy of Sura (second half of the ninth century), states that at the end of the year of mourning

---

[1] *Nedarim* 12a; *Yevamot* 122a and Rashi *ad. loc*; *Shevuot* 20a.

they were accustomed to say *Hashkavah* ('Laying to rest').

Although the anniversary of a death is known to have been observed in Biblical times, the term by which the institution is now widely known is mediaeval and was first used by Rabbi Moses Minz, a fifteenth-century scholar.[1] It is the *Ashkenazim* who call it *Yahrzeit*, whereas among the *Sephardim* it is called *Nachalah Meldado*, or *Annos*.

Yahrzeit is observed on the Jewish date on which the parent died. If death took place after dark, it must be dated from the next civil day as the day is reckoned among Jews from sunset to sunset.[2] According to some Rabbinic authorities if three or more days elapse between death and burial, the first *Yahrzeit* is observed on the date of burial. Subsequently *Yahrzeit* is observed on the anniversary of the day of death. But 'it has never been customary under the jurisdiction of the Chief Rabbi of the United Hebrew Congregations of the British Commonwealth to observe the *Yahrzeit* after the death on the anniversary of the burial as is enjoined, in certain circumstances, by some authorities.'[3] If death took place during *Adar* I or *Adar* II, i.e. in a leap year, *Yahrzeit* is observed in a leap year in the same *Adar* in which the death took place. If death occurred in the month of *Adar* in an ordinary year, the *Yahrzeit* is observed on the first *Adar* of a leap year but *Kaddish* may be recited in *Adar Sheni*.

A difficulty arises in connection with a death occurring on the last day of the months of *Cheshvan* or *Kislev* in the years when they have 30 days. In some years these months contain only 29 days and in such circumstances, the *Yahrzeit* for a person who died on the 30th of *Cheshvan* or *Kislev* is observed on the first of

---

[1] Zimmels, *op. cit.* p. 186, note 5. *Responsa* No. 80, also R. Isaac of Tyrnau in J.E. vii, p. 64.

[2] It is based on the story of the Creation. 'It was evening, it was morning the first day' (Gen. i: 5); the evening came first.

[3] *The Jewish Year Book* (1964), p. 29.

Kislev or first of *Tevet* as the case may be.[1]

In cases of doubt as to the exact day of death, for example in the case of relatives of the six million Jews murdered by the Nazis, the bereaved may select an appropriate day of the Jewish calendar and observe it as the *Yahrzeit* in all successive years.

The mourner's *Kaddish* should be recited at every Service during the day, a custom which is mentioned by Rabbi Isaac b. Moses of Vienna (ca. 1250) in his ritual code *Or Zarua*: 'For the recital of *Kaddish*' say the Cabbalists 'elevates the soul every year to a higher sphere in Paradise.'[2]

Normally the mourner conducts the Service if he is able to, and if circumstances permit. On the Sabbath before the *Yahrzeit* he should be called up to the Reading of the Law and if possible should recite *Haftarah*.[3] This practice is derived from an ancient Synagogue ritual when the words, 'O, faithful God who sayest and doest, who speaketh and ful-

---

[1] i.e. If a person died on *Rosh Chodesh Kislev*, when there is only one day *Rosh Chodesh*, the *Yahrzeit* should be observed in a year when there are two days *Rosh Chodesh Kislev* on the second day of *Rosh Chodesh* (which will be the first day of *Kislev*), since this was the date of death. If, however, he died on the first day of *Rosh Chodesh Kislev* (when it was two days *Rosh Chodesh*), then in the year when there is only one day *Rosh Chodesh Kislev*, the *Yahrzeit* should be observed on the 29th of *Cheshvan*. If, however, in the first anniversary there are two days *Rosh Chodesh*, he should keep the *Yahrzeit* on the first day of *Rosh Chodesh* and in that case he is considered to have established the precedent of observing the *Yahrzeit* on *Rosh Chodesh* and he must continue to keep it on *Rosh Chodesh* in all succeeding years, even in a year when there is only one day *Rosh Chodesh*. One who has *Yahrzeit* on any of the days of *Chanukah*, which happen to coincide with *Rosh Chodesh Tevet* or any of the days following *Rosh Chodesh*, should be careful not to count the *Yahrzeit* according to the particular days of *Chanukah*. The dates of the days of *Chanukah* in *Tevet* vary as to whether there are one or two days *Rosh Chodesh*.

[2] Isaac Luria, see Abraham Lewysohn, *op. cit.*

[3] Lit. 'Conclusion'. The portion selected from the books of the Prophets and read after the Reading of the Law.

fillest all whose words are truth and righteousness'[1] were chanted by the one who read the *Haftarah*, and the congregation responded 'Faithful art Thou, O Lord our God.'

A Memorial Prayer is offered on the previous Sabbath in memory of the deceased, and the mourner in some congregations officiates at the Evening Service at the end of the Sabbath.

It is a well-established custom to visit the grave on the *Yahrzeit*. 'I have seen in the *Responsa* of the *Geonim*,' writes Rashi[2], 'that on the anniversary of the death people assemble around the grave and hold a discourse and offer a prayer.'

MEMORIAL LIGHT

It was a well-established practice to have a candle or lamp burning in the home throughout the twenty-four hours of the anniversary of the death of a departed parent or relative,[3] although no authority for this is found in the Talmud or *Midrash*.

Many reasons for this custom have been suggested. Light, for instance, symbolises the soul and suggests human immortality. 'The soul of man,' says the Book of Proverbs, 'is the lamp of the Lord' (xx: 27). Also the mystics have pointed out that the numerical value of the letters of the Hebrew phrase *Ner Daluk* (a kindled light) and the Hebrew word *Hashechinah* (the Divine Presence) add up to 390.[4]

Others give a different reason. In the Pentateuchal portion *Tezaveh* (Ex. xxvii: 20-xxx: 10), which is read during the week of the 7th *Adar*, the traditional date for commemorating Moses' death, the opening verse states that the children of Israel were commanded 'to bring pure olive oil beaten for the light to cause a lamp to burn continually' (Ex. xxvii: 20).

[1] A.P.B. p. 199.
[2] Rashi, *Yevamot* 122a.
[3] *Leket Yosher I*, p. 49. See Zimmels, *op. cit.* p. 187.
[4] *Maavar Yabok*, xv.94b.

FASTING

Fasting was closely associated with mourning in the Bible[1] and also in the Apocrypha where we read that Judith fasted every day except Friday and Saturday while she was mourning. The Talmud considers the validity of a vow by a man who says: 'I am not to eat meat or drink wine on the day that my father or teacher died.'[2] From this we gather that it was the custom to fast on the anniversary of the death of a parent. But this was not done if it was a day on which *Tachanun* is not said. The *Kol Bo*[3] cites the authority of R. Meir b. Baruch of Rothenburg (a 13th-century scholar) for the antiquity of this custom. 'It is a religious duty to fast on the day that one's father or mother died.'

Rabbi Israel Baal Shem Tov (1700–1760) maintains that on the day of the *Yahrzeit* God judges the soul which is in the upper world and so, when a son fasts, he brings honour to his departed parent. Fasting is an expression of repentance and atonement, a mark of reverence for the departed and an act of humiliation before God.

If the *Yahrzeit* falls on the day before or after a public fast, and the mourner is unable to fast on two consecutive days, he should observe the public fast and fast only until noon on the day of the *Yahrzeit*.

If the *Sandek* or the *Mohel* should happen to have *Yahrzeit* for a parent on the day of a *Brit Milah*, they may not fast. Nor does the father of a first-born or the Cohen from whom the latter is redeemed fast if they observe *Yahrzeit* on the day of the Redemption of the first-born.[4] A bride or bridegroom does not fast if *Yahrzeit* occurs during the seven days of marriage festivities.[5] If a man

---

[1] I Sam. xxxi: 13, II Sam. 1: 12, Joel 1: 17, Zech. vii: 4–7, vii: 9.

[2] *Nedarim* 12a.

[3] Lit. 'Compendium'. Name of a medieval Jewish legal codification often ascribed to either Rabbi Joseph b. Tobais or Rabbi Shemaryah b. Simchah.

[4] *Kitzur Shulchan Aruch* 221.6.

[5] *Ibid.*

has fasted once on a *Yahrzeit*, he should fast every year.[1]

STUDY AND CHARITY

On *Yahrzeit* a man ought to set aside a certain time for study, and should also distribute money to worthy causes. 'Forgive O Lord, thy people Israel, whom Thou hast redeemed, and suffer not innocent blood to remain in the midst of Thy people Israel' (Deut. xxi: 8) pleaded the Elders of Israel. This is interpreted to mean that the dead need atonement and the living can atone for them by means of charity. 'Such is the power of charity that it can deliver a sinner from the punishment of *Gehenna*.'[2]

It is customary to study parts of the *Mishnah*, for the Hebrew word for soul (*Neshamah*) has the same letters as *Mishnah*. The passages chosen are the twenty-fourth chapter of *Kelim*[3] and the fourth chapter of *Mikvaot* (Immersion pools) from the sixth and last Order (*Seder*) of the *Mishnah Tohorot*.[4]

If one has been unable to recite *Kaddish* on the *Yahrzeit* day, then he may say *Kaddish* at the *Maariv* (Evening) service following the day of the *Yahrzeit*.

Amusements should be avoided on the day of the *Yahrzeit*. One may not on the evening when the *Yahrzeit* is observed eat at a marriage feast that has musical entertainment. One may, however, eat at a feast held in connection with a circumcision or a redemption of a first-born or at the conclusion of a Talmudic tractate.[5]

CHASSIDIC CUSTOMS

Among the Cabbalists the day of the *Yahrzeit* is regarded

[1] Y.D. 376.4; Danzig, *Chochmat Adam*, 171.

[2] *Baba Batra*, 10a.

[3] Lit. Vessels. This chapter has seventeen *Mishnayot* numerically equal to the Hebrew word *Tov* (good).

[4] Lit. 'purity'. The name is a euphemism for ritual uncleanliness, and all the treatises of the Order deal with the laws concerning impurity.

[5] *Kitzur Shulchan Aruch* 221.7 and *Pitche Teshuvah*.

as a 'marriage,' a blissful reunion of the soul with the *Shechinah* (Divine Presence). One outstanding celebration is the *Yahrzeit* of the *Tanna* and mystic Rabbi Simon bar Yochai (ca. 130–160). On *Lag Ba'Omer*,[1] thousands of Israelis converge on the white tomb at Meron (Upper Galilee) when at midnight the *hadlakah* (bonfire) is lit, as a sign for the celebrations to begin. This pilgrimage to Meron is an old tradition which Rabbi Isaac ben Solomon Luria (1534–1572) observed. His disciple Rabbi Chayyim Vital (1543–1620) wrote: 'In these last eight years my teacher, his wife and family have gone there and they stay for three days.'[2] *Ashkenazim* and *Sephardim*, *Chassidim* and *Mitnagdim*, *Sabras* and Yemenites all go to Meron, where they recite Psalms and quote passages from the *Zohar*.

This holy place attracts the mystic, the pious, the poor, the sick and the anxious and on arrival, these spectators become participants and all share in a moving experience. The pilgrims dance and pray at the same time, inspired with *hitlahabut*—religious ecstasy (not riotous revelry), a spirit of awe (not light-hearted gaiety). As the flames mount higher, the words of the song can be heard: 'Bar Yochai, Bar Yochai, Happy one, anointed with oil of joy, blessed by the mouth of God, blessed from the day of Creation.'

Though Rabbi Israel Baal Shem Tov instructed his followers to fast on a *Yahrzeit*, most *Chassidim* follow the tradition of Rabbi Dov Baer, the Maggid of Messeritz (d. 1772) who advised his *Chassidim* 'not to fast but to make a *Seudah* and distribute money to charity.' It is customary among the *Chassidim*, inspired by their enthusiasm and ecstasy, to sing and even to dance at such a *Seudah* and say 'The soul should have an *Aliyah*' (May the soul of the deceased be raised to a still higher level of purity).

The phrase which is popular in the English-speaking world, 'I wish you long life,' can be traced back to the

[1] The thirty-third day of the *Omer*, corresponding to the 18th day of *Iyar*.
[2] *Etz Chayyim* 22; *Sephirat Haomer* 7.

Midrash.[1] 'In ordinary cases,' states the *Midrash*, 'where a man's son dies, people say to him, to comfort him, "May your other son who is left you live"; and if he has no other son they say "We wish you long life." '

MEMORIAL SERVICES

It is customary to recite *Yizkor* ('May God remember the soul of my revered . . .')[2] four times during the year: on *Yom Kippur*, on the eighth day of *Sukkot* (*Shemini Atzeret*), on the last day of Passover and on the second day of *Shavuot* (Pentecost). *Yizkor* is generally not recited during the first twelve months after the death of parents.

In some congregations, those whose parents are alive leave the Synagogue during *Yizkor*. The object of this may be either to leave the mourners undisturbed during this moving prayer, or to spare those who have not been bereaved any unnecessary grief. All too often this results in an untidy and indecorous general exit which lowers the dignity of the service.

It is difficult to establish with any degree of certainty when *Yizkor* became customary in the Synagogue.

In the second book of Maccabees (xii: 43–45) we read that Judas collected two thousand drachmas of silver and sent it to Jerusalem as a sin-offering for those who had died 'in that he was mindful of the resurrection. For if he had not hoped that they that were slain should have risen again, it had been superfluous and vain to pray for the dead. And also in that he perceived that there was great favour laid up for those that died godly, it was an holy and good thought. Whereupon he made a reconciliation for the dead, that they might be delivered from sin.'

Rabbi Simchah ben Samuel of Vitry (d. 1105) in his liturgical work *Machzor Vitry*, Rabbi Joseph Caro,[3] and Rabbi Moses Isserles all refer to the practice of pledging

[1] *Midrash Rabbah*, Esther VIII: 2.
[2] A.P.B. p. 436.
[3] *Orach Chayyim* 621.5.

alms on the Day of Atonement. 'On *Yom Kippur* the names of the dead should be mentioned, for they too may obtain atonement.' Some explained the plural term *Kippurim* as denoting atonement for the living and the dead.[1] Furthermore, mention of the departed makes man humble and subdues his evil impulses.

Later, *Yizkor* was also recited on the last day of Passover, the second day of Pentecost and on the eighth day of Tabernacles, appropriate days on which to give charity on behalf of the living and in memory of the departed. For on these three Festivals, the Reading of the Law (Deut. XIV: 22–XVI: 17) includes the verse: 'Every man shall give as he is able, according to the blessing of the Lord thy God which he hath given thee.'

The recital of the names of the dead in the Synagogue probably began at the time of the Crusades, which brought death and desolation to the flourishing and ancient Jewish communities on the Rhine and the Moselle. The names of the martyrs who died for the 'Sanctification of God's Name' were inscribed in special books known as *Memorbucher* (Memorial Books) or *Sepher Zikaron* (Book of Remembrance), or *Sepher Zikronot Neshamot* (Memorial Book of the Souls).[2] One of the earliest of these books was begun at Nuremberg in 1296 and it served as a model for other communities. The martyrs' names were read during the *Omer* period, on the Sabbath before Pentecost and on the Sabbath preceding the 9th of *Av*.

The Requiem for the Martyrs, 'May the Father of mercies' (*Av Harachamim*)[3] is said nowadays in western countries on the Sabbaths preceding Pentecost and the 9th of *Av*. It was the Polish *Minhag* (custom) to recite it

---

[1] Jacob Weil (15th century) quoted by Eisenstein, *Ozar Dinim Uminhagim* p. 97; *Machzor Vitry*, pp. 173, 392; *Sepher He-Chassidim* 1171–2; *Siddur Rashi* 214.

[2] J.E. Vol. VIII, p. 456.

[3] A.P.B. p. 155. It was probably composed during the first Crusade in 1096.

every Sabbath except on days when *Tachanun* would be omitted on a weekday.

EL MALE RACHAMIM

The prayer, 'O God who art full of compassion, who dwellest on high,'[1] is not found in the Codes or in the works of Rabbi Jacob b. Asher (1269–1343), author of the *Arbaah Turim*. Probably seventeenth-century in origin, it is mentioned by Rabbi Naphtali Herz in *Bet Hillel* and by Rabbi Joseph ben Meir Teomim and is recited on Sabbaths and Festivals.

There is no basis for the idea that one should not offer prayers for the dead on the Sabbath. The *Midrash* states: 'Therefore, it is a custom to mention the dead on Sabbath in order that they should not return to Gehenna.'[2] Rabbi Moses Isserles quotes Zedekiah b. Abraham Anav (13th century), author of *Shibbole Haleket* as follows: 'After the reading of the Torah, it is customary to recite Memorial Prayers.[3] This is not regarded as lamentation which is forbidden on a Sabbath.' In his Ethical Will, Rabbi Nathaniel son of Benjamin Trabotti (1576–1658) writes: 'Moreover, I entreat you to offer up a memorial for my soul every Sabbath day and I from my grave will always be mindful of you, praying to God on your behalf.'[4]

The *Sephardim* recite *Hashkavah* (Laying to rest) on Sabbath, festivals or on Mondays or Thursdays. The prayer is as follows: 'A good name is more fragrant than rich perfume; and the day of death better than the day of one's birth. The sum of the matter, after all hath been heard, is to fear God and keep His commandments, for this is the whole of man. Let the pious be joyful in glory; let them sing aloud upon their couches. May the repose which is prepared in the celestial abode, under the wings of the Divine

[1] A.P.B. p. 423.
[2] *Tanchumah Yelamdenu Haazinu* and *Kol Bo*.
[3] *Orach Chayyim* 284.7 (*Rema*).
[4] I. Abrahams, *Hebrew Ethical Wills*, Vol. II, p. 276.

Presence in the high places of the holy and pure—that shine and are resplendent as the brightness of the firmament—with a renewal of strength, a forgiveness of trespasses, a removal of transgressions, an approach of salvation, compassion and favour from Him that sitteth enthroned on high, and also a goodly portion in the life to come, be the lot, dwelling and the resting place of the soul of our deceased brother . . .'[1]

The *El Male Rachamim*[2] (O Lord who art full of compassion) may also be said several times at the cemetery, provided that each time it is accompanied by alms giving, for 'Charity delivereth from death.' 'Unless we are prepared to maintain,' wrote the Rev. Simeon Singer (1846–1906) 'that at his death the fate of man is fixed irretrievably and for ever; that, therefore, the sinner who rejected much of God's love during a brief lifetime, has lost all of it eternally —prayer for the peace and salvation of the departed soul commends itself as one of the highest religious obligations.'[3]

'The Memorial Service is primarily dedicated to those of our own family who have been called to life eternal; but it also recalls those countless Jews who were murderously cut down because they were Jews. Aspects of the *Yizkor* service can be traced to the days of the torturing martyrdom suffered by our forefathers in the time of the Crusades. In our own generation these memorial prayers have all too tragically become prayers through which anyone who bears the name Jew can pour out his soul in lamentation for the millions of his fellow Jews who after foulest torture met their end in death chambers and organised massacre. Each of us standing in the Synagogue can and should passionately exclaim: 'In their memory I offer charity and would do good." [4]

---

[1] Gaster, *The Book of Prayer and Order of Service according to the custom of the Spanish and Portuguese Jews.* Vol. I. (London, 1901), pp. 200–201.
[2] A.P.B. p. 423.
[3] J. H. Hertz, *Daily Prayer Book*, pp. 1094–5.
[4] David De Sola Pool, *The Traditional Prayer Book*, p. 474.

CHAPTER

X

THE TOMBSTONE (*MATZEVAH*)

It is customary to erect a tombstone on the grave of a departed. In modern times, the ceremony of consecrating the tombstone is the climax of the year of mourning and has great significance for the mourners. A special Consecration Service is held at which suitable Psalms are recited and a Memorial Address is often given. Finally the inscription is read and *Kaddish* is recited.

The Bible relates that Jacob 'set up a pillar upon her grave; the same is the pillar of Rachel's grave unto this day' (Gen. xxxv: 20). Later it is stated that Absalom, too, built a monument in the valley of Kidron 'to keep his name in remembrance' (II Sam. xviii: 18). Many such memorials have survived, notably the tomb of King David in Jerusalem, the tomb of Rachel at Beth Lechem, the tombs of the Patriarchs in Hebron as well as the resting places of many famous Rabbis in Israel.

From the Biblical period and the time when the practice of erecting tombstones became general, it was the custom simply to pile up stones or place a distinctive sign on the site of a grave, or set up pillars as memorials.[1] This served the two-fold purpose of protecting the body from wild beasts and of indicating to passers-by and especially priests (*Cohanim*) that a grave was there. The *Mishnah* reports that on the 15th of *Adar* the graves were painted white to warn people of the existence of a grave so that they might avoid

---

[1] Ezek. xxxix: 15; II Kings xxiii: 17; II Sam. xviii: 17.

becoming unclean by contact with it.[1] Rabbi Nathan lays down that 'the surplus of any money collected to pay for the burial of the dead should be used to build a monument over the grave.'[2]

Yet it was not until the Greek period that we begin to find evidence of the erection of lavish monuments. Simon Maccabaeus (d. 135 B.C.E.) son of Mattathias the Hasmonean, and brother of Judah, put up a most elaborate mausoleum for his father and his brothers at Modin. 'Simon,' records the First Book of Maccabees (xiii: 27–29) 'built a monument upon the sepulchre of his father and his brethren, and raised it aloft to the sight with polished stone behind and before. And he set up seven pyramids, one over against another, for his father, and his mother, and his four brethren. And for these he made cunning devices setting about them great pillars, and upon the pillars he fashioned all manner of arms for a perpetual memory, and beside the arms carved ships, that they should be seen of all that sail on the sea.' Josephus, too, mentions the monuments on the graves of John Hyrcanus, Alexander Janneus, and Queen Helena of Adiabene.[3]

SECOND BURIAL

In Talmudic times often when the burial chamber became crowded, the relatives removed the decomposed body and placed the bones in a stone coffin known as an ossuary. The Talmud and Codes lay down minute regulations for the one 'who collects bones for final burial.'[4] The late Professor Eliezer Lipa Sukenik (1889–1953) excavated a number of these ossuaries in Israel. Many bore inscriptions in Hebrew, Aramaic or Greek. Among the engravings were the *Menorah* (Candelabrum), the *Shophar* (a ram's horn) and the phrase 'Peace upon Israel.'

[1] *Shekalim* i: 1; *Moed Katan* 6a.
[2] *Shekalim* ii: 5.
[3] Ant. xiii.6.6; xvi.7.i; xx.4.3; Wars v.6.2.
[4] Y.D.403, 1–10.

The Jews in Rome had their renowned catacombs.[1] Of the many inscriptions that have so far been deciphered, one is in Aramaic, another in both Greek and Aramaic, ten contain the Hebrew word *Shalom* and the rest are entirely in Greek or in Latin. There, too, we find familiar symbols: the *Shophar*, the *etrog* (citron), the seven branched candlestick, the trumpets, the scroll as well as the unfamiliar pictorial representation of human figures.

It is patently clear that, apart from isolated instances, the Jews in the first eight or nine centuries of the Common Era used the dominant language, Greek or Latin, for their funerary inscriptions. Hebrew gradually superseded them and in the tenth century inscriptions written entirely in Hebrew are found in Spain, France and many other countries.

ANCIENT TOMBSTONES

Rabbi Moses ben Nachman (1194–1270) relates that in Spain the graves were protected by heaps of stones, though these failed to prevent frequent desecrations. Menachem (Immanuel) Azariah da Fano (1548–1620) complains that 'we are persecuted by men bent on stealing the stones and using them in the construction of their theatres (Churches) or for sepulchres for their own dead.'[2] Few of the ancient graves remained intact or have been preserved. Among the oldest tombstones extant are one in Prague going back to 606, one in Breslau dated 1044 and one in Mayence, on the tomb of Rabbi Kalonymos ben Meshullam, dated 1096. Today, few ancient graves remain intact in Europe, mainly because during the Nazi holocaust most of the historic Jewish cemeteries were wantonly destroyed. Only a few stones miraculously survived the barbaric vandalism.

[1] H. J. Leon, 'New Material about the Jews of Ancient Rome' in *Jewish Quarterly Review*, xx 1929–1930, pp. 301–312.
[2] S. W. Baron, *The Jewish Community*, II, p. 151.

THE TOMBSTONE (MATZEVAH)

TIME FOR CONSECRATION

It was formerly the practice for the tombstone to be erected as soon as possible after the *Shivah*. More recently it has become the custom to allow a year to elapse and not to erect the stone until the first *Yahrzeit* or during the week of the *Yahrzeit*.

The stone should be simple to emphasise that in death 'rich and poor meet together' (Prov. xxII: 2). Many scholars left precise instructions for simple gravestones to be erected. Expensive tombstones have always been considered ostentatious. In orthodox circles it is felt that they may undermine belief in the coming of the Messiah and the resurrection.

The *Ashkenazim* place their tombstones upright while the *Sephardim* lay them horizontally on the graves. A Levite's gravestone often bears a ewer as a symbol of his office in the Temple, that of serving the priests. The tombs of priests (*Cohanim*) are marked by a carving of the hands as raised in the Priestly Benediction. In some continental communities various emblems representing the professions of the deceased and family coats of arms were carved on the stone. It is customary in many communities, especially among the *Chassidim*, to construct a sepulchre (*Ohel*) over the grave of a *Zaddik* which often became a place of pilgrimage. The materials used for tombstones were generally stone, marble or granite.

INSCRIPTIONS

There is no uniform practice with regard to the inscription on a stone. No inscriptions existed in Biblical times. In the first century of the common era, the epitaph had the words *Berabbi* or *Beribbi* (Son of the teacher), *Zichrono* (*ah*) *Livrachah* (May his (her) memory be a blessing), *Zechur Letov* (May he be remembered for good'), *Shalom* (Peace) and *Noach nephesh* (repose to his soul).

In mediaeval times long eulogies or laments were often added to the name of the deceased, as well as details of his character, his deeds and his life. Elaborate inscriptions were usual for the tombs of scholars and Rabbis. Many Rabbis composed in advance the epitaphs which they desired to be put on their tombstones. The inscription on the stone of the Talmudist and Cabbalist Rabbi Jonathan Eibeschutz (c. 1690–1764) reads as follows: 'Every passer-by should see what is engraved on these tables. The man who stood as a model, who flourished like a lily, returned to dust, and his visage became marred more than any man's. Pray, take it to heart to repent sincerely and to offer for him many prayers to the Lord of spirits that He should gather to Him his soul and not cast it away. The merit of your deeds will be a protection, for all the souls of Israel are one. Learn to despise honours and to flee from greatness.'[1]

Of great interest is the epitaph of Urania of Worms, belonging to the 13th century, which reads: 'This headstone commemorates the eminent and excellent Lady Urania, the daughter of R. Abraham, who was the chief of the Synagogue singers. His prayer for his people rose up unto glory. And as for her, with sweet tunefulness officiated before the female worshippers, to whom she sang the hymnal portions. In devout service her memory shall be preserved.'[2]

Nor was there any uniform practice with regard to the language used on a stone. The tombstones in the *Sephardi* cemetery in London in the 18th century were inscribed partly in Hebrew and partly in Spanish or Portuguese. An 18th-century writer throws some light on the *Ashkenazi* usage. 'In the cemetery belonging to the Dutch Jews, the rows are not kept so regularly, and the tombs resemble more than in our burial grounds. The inscriptions are entirely Hebrew . . . The Dutch Jews are equally averse from disturbing the bones of the dead, and if the cemetery is full, they cover it with a stratum of earth of sufficient

---

[1] *The Jewish Encyclopedia* XII, p. 193.
[2] Israel Abrahams, *op. cit.* p. 40.

depth to make fresh graves, but the Portuguese always purchase new ground.'[1]

Nowadays communities lay down their own regulations regarding the nature of the inscriptions and in some cases even of the tombstones. In *Ashkenazi* cemeteries it is customary to place the letters פ׳נ נָטְמָן פֹּה. 'Here lies buried' for a male and פֹּה טְמוּנָה ט׳ס . 'Here lies hidden' for a female. The *Sephardim*, however, use the letters מ׳ק מַצֶּבֶת קְבוּרַת 'The tombstone of the grave' for both sexes.

Some ultra-Orthodox communities permit only Hebrew inscriptions.[2] It is forbidden to place a likeness of the deceased on the grave.

The tendency today is for short epitaphs. All that is generally engraved on a tombstone is the name of the deceased both in Hebrew and English, together with the dates of birth and death, usually also in Hebrew with the Hebrew consonants of ת״נ״צ״ב״ה (*Tehe nishmoso zerurah bitzror hachayyim*), 'May his soul be bound up in the bond of eternal life.'

TOMBSTONE CONSECRATION

As with the inscription, the form of consecration service tends to vary. In Eastern Europe, even in modern times, there was no special form of service. Psalms were chanted and *Kaddish* was recited and the duty of the mourner was discharged without formula or formality.

In western lands it has become customary to follow a

[1] *Laws and Bye-laws of the Burial Society*, p. 16; Also Cecil Roth, *History of the Great Synagogue*, London, p. 103.

[2] *The Laws and Bye-laws of the Burial Society of the United Synagogue* states, 'The propriety and orthography of inscriptions and of designs and emblems on a tombstone shall be subject to the approval of the Treasurers, whose decision shall be final. The name in Hebrew of the deceased and the Hebrew ת״נ״צ״ב״ה (or שָׁלוֹם.) must form part of every inscription. The dates according to the Jewish and Civil eras shall be permitted in the inscription.' (G.49, p. 70).

special order of service in which Psalms I, XVI, XXIII and other appropriate passages are read.[1] The first Psalm, 'Happy is the man that walketh not in the counsel of the wicked nor standeth in the way of sinners, nor sitteth in the seat of the scornful. But his delight is in the law of the Lord; and in his law doth he meditate day and night,' is an appropriate theme for the service. Sometimes verses from Psalm CXIX, which consists of twenty-two stanzas (corresponding to the number of letters in the Hebrew alphabet), are recited. Appropriate stanzas are chosen to correspond with the Hebrew name of the deceased. It is also usual to pay a modest tribute to the departed. An address should not be delivered on a day when *Tachanun* is not said. Tombstones should not be consecrated on *Chol Hamoed*, *Purim*, or on *Tisha B'Av*.

Although in some circles attendance of women at funerals is discouraged or forbidden, women do attend tombstone consecrations.

One may take a photograph of the tombstone.[2] One may not in any way make use of or derive any profit from a disused tombstone.

Tombstone inscriptions are, of course, a valuable source of socio-historical information. They are also rich in ethical values. Particularly inspiring, for example, is the writing on the tombstone at Middleburg, Holland, of the Dutch Rabbi Manasseh ben Israel (1604–1657): 'The Rabbi did not die; his light is not yet extinguished; he liveth still in the heights of the All Revered. By his pen and the sweetness of his speech his remembrance will be eternal like the days of the earth.'[3]

---

[1] A.P.B. pp. 434–435.
[2] Greenwald, *op. cit.* p. 384.
[3] *The Jewish Encyclopedia*, XII, p. 192.

CHAPTER

XI

THE UNDISCOVERED COUNTRY

THIS little book, which describes the rites and customs of
mourning, would be incomplete without some mention of
the Jewish approach to the hereafter. At the same time, it
should be pointed out that Judaism does not encourage too
much probing in this subject. 'Such knowledge,' says the
Psalmist, 'is too wonderful for me; too high, I cannot attain
unto it' (cxxxix:6). Judaism discourages the attempts to seek
through mystical practices release from the chains of the
physical world. Indeed it proved dangerous for the four
Sages who penetrated the *Pardes*[1] (the realm of mysteries)
since only Rabbi Akiva (ca. 50–137) entered and returned
safely. Simon ben Azzai (early second century) died, Simon
ben Zoma lost his senses, and Elisha ben Avuyah, the col-
league of Rabbi Akiva, became an apostate. It is thus not
surprising that the Rabbis approved on Ben Sira's stern
warning, 'Seek not things that are too hard for thee and
search not out things that are above thy strength.'[2]

Among believers in Judaism there have always been
ascetics, such as the Nazirites,[3] the Essenes, the Dead Sea
Community, and all the fasting mystics, who despised the
physical delights of the world. They, however, are the exception. Self-mortification, celibacy and asceticism have
never been regarded by the Sages as essential to entering
the Kingdom of Heaven. 'In the hereafter,' warned the

[1] *Chagigah*, 14*b*.
[2] *Ecclesiasticus* III: 2.
[3] Num. VI: 1–21.

121

Sages, 'a man will have to give account for the permissible pleasures from which he has abstained.'[1]

Judaism has never retreated from life. Indeed, even the author of Ecclesiastes, the greatest of all pessimists, conceded: 'I know that there is nothing better for them than to rejoice, and to get pleasure so long as they live. But also that every man should eat and drink, and enjoy pleasure for all his labour, is the gift of God' (III: 12–13).

On the other hand, the hedonist philosophy of 'eat, drink and be merry, for tomorrow we die' is alien and abhorrent to Judaism.

Although the period of man's life on earth is limited, it has a definite part in the divine providence and scheme of history. In the words of John Macmurray:[2] 'Jewish reflection thinks of history as the act of God. Where our historians say "Caesar crossed the Rubicon," or "Nelson won the Battle of Trafalgar," the Jewish historian says, "God brought His people up out of the land of Egypt." '

Judaism rejects both the Hegelian approach to history and the dialectical materialism of Karl Marx. To Jews, God is the Lord of history controlling the destiny of man from the cradle to the grave and beyond.

Unlike the ancient Egyptians, who were as much preoccupied with death as with life and therefore filled their tombs with precious stones and utensils and provisions for life after death of the departed, the Hebrews believed that 'in the hour of man's departure from this world, neither silver nor gold nor precious stones nor pearls accompany him, but only Torah and good works.'[3]

'While you do not know life, what can you know about death?' demanded Confucius. The Rabbis, too, asked this unanswerable question, maintaining that man could not comprehend the mystery of immortality.

'Know that just as a blind man,' reasons Maimonides,

---

[1] *Yerushalmi* end of *Kiddushin.*
[2] *The Clue to History,* p. 30.
[3] *Avot* VI: 9.

'can form no idea of colours, nor a deaf man comprehend sounds . . . so the body cannot comprehend the delights of the soul. Even as fish do not know the element of fire because they exist ever in the opposite, so are the delights of the world of the spirit unknown in this world of the flesh. Indeed, we have no pleasure in any way except what is bodily and what the sense can comprehend of eating and drinking. Whatever is outside these is non-existent to us. We do not discern it, neither do we grasp it at first thought, but only after deep penetration.

And truly, this must necessarily be the case. For we live in a material world and the only pleasure we can comprehend must be material. But the delights of the spirit are everlasting and uninterrupted, and there is no resemblance in any possible way between spiritual and bodily enjoyments.'[1]

Science cannot solve the riddle of the 'undiscovered country from whose bourne no traveller returns.' Judaism does not agree with the philosophy of Martin Heidegger, that man is dedicated to death for which he has a genuine instinct, nor with that of Epicurus: 'While we live, death is absent, and when we die we are absent, so death is simply non-existent for us.'

But Judaism, although primarily concerned with the miracle of life, does not ignore the mystery of death, and from Biblical and Rabbinic literature it is possible to suggest the nature of the hereafter.

THE SOUL

The soul is known as *Neshamah*, *Nephesh* or *Ruach* (breath)[2] and is the source without which there can be no life. 'O Lord my God,' entreated the prophet Elijah, 'I pray Thee, let this child's soul come back into him.' And the Lord hearkened unto the voice of Elijah; and the soul

[1] Maimonides, Commentary on the *Mishnah*, Introduction to *Sanhedrin* x.

[2] Also known as *Yechidah* ('the only one') and *Chayyah* ('living being'), *Midrash Genesis Rabbah* xiv.9.

123

of the child came back into him and he revived' (I Kings
XVII: 21–22). The soul originated with God (Gen. II: 17)
and is a gift to man. 'It is the lamp of God which He hath
breathed into man. It must thus remain in its state and
cannot die . . . its continued existence being natural and
enduring for ever.'[1]

Before the body came into being, the soul already existed,[2]
and has done so since the beginning of time. The souls of
all men are in the hands of the Holy One, blessed be He,
and are not in any way tainted by 'original sin.' Every
morning of the year, the faithful Jew prays: "O my God,
the soul which thou gavest me is pure; thou didst create it,
thou didst form it, thou didst breathe it into me; thou
preservest it within me; and thou wilt take it from me, but
wilt restore it unto me hereafter. So long as the soul is
within me, I will give thanks unto thee." '[3]

Some believed that the soul is diffused throughout the
body. 'Just as the Holy One, blessed be He, He sees, but
is not seen, so the soul sees but is not itself seen. Just as the
Holy One, blessed be He, feeds the whole world, so the soul
feeds the whole body. Just as the Holy One, blessed be He,
is pure, so the soul is pure.'[4] Other sages held that the exact
dwelling place of the soul could be determined. 'You want
to know,' said Rabban Gamaliel, 'the dwelling place
of God who is so distant from us: your body is very
close to you, yet can you tell in what part of it is
your soul?'[5]

RETRIBUTION

'Judgment for an evil thing,' says Carlyle, 'is many times
delayed, sometimes a day or two, sometimes a century or

[1] Moses Nachmanides.
[2] *Chagigah* 12b.
[3] A.P.B. p. 6; *Berachot* 60b.
[4] *Ibid*, 10a.
[5] *Midrash Tehillim* (*Shocher Tov*), ed. S. Buber (Vilna, 1891),
Psalm 103, p. 433.

two, but it is as sure as life, it is as sure as death.' This is also one of the beliefs of Judaism, where not only is it laid down that 'the wicked shall die in his iniquity' (Ezek. III: 18), but also that 'with what measure a man metes it shall be measured to him again.'[1]

A man's deeds during his lifetime vindicate the saint and entitle him to enter Heaven, but they destroy the sinner so that he is rejected. For the Almighty faithfully punishes the wicked and rewards the righteous, if not in this world, then in the world to come. This belief is one of Maimonides' Thirteen Articles of Faith. 'I believe with perfect faith,' the Jew declares, 'that the Creator Blessed be His name, rewards those that keep His commandments, and punishes those that transgress them.'[2] The Rabbis stress that 'it is not in our power to explain either the prosperity of the wicked or the afflictions of the righteous.'[3] Belief in the existence of another world, the world of Truth, and Justice and Mercy, is the Jewish explanation of the seeming inequalities and inconsistencies of this life.

GEHENNA AND GAN EDEN

Rabbi Joshua ben Levi lists seven Biblical names for Hell (*Gehenna*): Nether-World, Destruction, Pit, Tumultuous Pit, Miry Clay, Shadow of Death and the Underworld.[4] The Bible occasionally refers to Hell, as in Job (X: 22) where it is 'a land of thick darkness, as darkness itself; a land of the shadow of death, without any order, and where the light is as darkness.' Jewish people generally call Hell *Ge-Hinnom* after the valley of Hinnom, a vale south-west of Jerusalem, where Solomon erected an altar to Moloch (I Kings XI: 7), and where Ahaz and Manasseh made their children 'pass through the fire.'[5] Eventually, the name of

---

[1] *Sotah* 1.7.
[2] A.P.B. p. 94.
[3] *Avot* IV.19.
[4] *Eruvin* 19a.
[5] II Kings XVI: 3 and XXI: 6.

this valley became for Jewish people synonymous with the legendary place of eternal torment.

Sheol is said to be an enormous land beneath the visible world, the home of the dead, where God's power is effective. 'But God will redeem my soul from the power of the nether-world; for He shall receive me' (Psalm XLIX: 16). There is no eternal punishment there, the maximum punishment being twelve months of penance and purification. 'For I am merciful, saith the Lord, I will not bear a grudge for ever' (Jer. III: 12).

This was not the only explanation of Hell. 'No purgatory,' says Rabbi Jacob Ha-Cohen of Polona (d. 1769), 'can be worse for the wicked than permission to enter the Garden of Eden. They find there no pleasure to which they were addicted in life; no eating or drinking or any other pleasures of the body. They see merely *Zaddikim*, deriving great joy from the nearness of the Lord. And who are these *Zaddikim* who occupy places of prominence in Paradise? They are the very persons upon whom the wicked poured out their scorn in life, and whose learning they thoroughly despised. What then, can these wicked persons feel in Paradise but bitterness? Can they know the joy of the *Shechinah's* nearness, inasmuch as they never trained themselves in their lifetime for the enjoyment of the spirit?'[1]

If, as the mystics say, body and soul are one, yet divisible and independent, how at the end shall man be judged? Which shall be answerable to the Divine Judge of Judges—the body, or the soul?

Antoninus (whom some identify with the Roman Emperor Marcus Aurelius),[2] once said to Rabbi Judah Hanasi:[3] 'On the great Day of Judgment, soul and body will each plead excuse for the sins that have been committed. The body will say to the Heavenly Judge, "It is the soul, and

[1] Louis Newman, *The Hasidic Anthology*, p. 3.
[2] Krauss identifies him with Avidius Cassius, general of Marcus Aurelius and a procurator of Judea.
[3] *Sanhedrin* 91a–b.

not I, that has sinned. Without it I am as lifeless as a stone."
On the other hand, the soul will say, "How canst Thou impute
sin to me? It is the body that has dragged me down." '

'Let me tell you a parable,' answered the Rabbi, 'A king
once had a beautiful garden stocked with the choicest fruits.
He set two men to keep guard over it—a blind man and a
lame man. "I see some fine fruit yonder" said the lame man
one day. "Come up on my shoulder" said the blind man.
"I will carry you to the spot, and we shall both enjoy the
fruit." The owner, missing the fruit, hauled both men before
him for punishment. "How could I have been the thief?"
said the lame man, "seeing that I cannot walk?" "Could I
have stolen the fruit?' retorted the blind man. 'I am
unable to see anything." What did the king do? He placed
the lame man on the shoulders of the blind man and sen-
tenced them both as one.'

In the same way, the Divine Judge of the Universe will
pass judgment on both body and soul together.

GAN EDEN

Virtue is its own reward. Nevertheless, the righteous are
constantly assured that they will be recompensed in Paradise. What is Paradise? It is known to us as Gan Eden (The
Garden of Eden) man's first home,[1] which was created even
before the world came into being, and has become by
tradition the eternal resting-place of the righteous.[2] 'Every
righteous person,' says the Talmud[3], 'will be assigned a
dwelling place in accordance with the honour due to him.
Remember the parable of a human king who entered a city
with servants. Although they all enter through one gate,
when they take up their quarters each is allotted a dwelling
place according to his rank.'

[1] Gen. II: 8.
[2] *Sifre*, Deut. 10.67; *Midrash* to Ps. XI.7.51a; *Yalkut Shimoni*
Genesis 20.
[3] *Shabbat* 152a. Cf. A. Cohen, *Everyman's Talmud*, London, 1943,
p. 408.

IMMORTALITY

Throughout the ages the question has been asked: 'If a man dies, will he live again?' Judaism replies emphatically that he will, and adds that this second life, the real life, will compensate for the imperfections of our brief earthly existence. 'But the souls of the righteous are in the hand of God, and no evil shall touch them ... For though in the sight of man they are punished, their hope is full of immortality.'[1]

The Jewish concept of immortality is purely spiritual, identifying the next world with the kingdom of God, the Most High, *Malchut Shadai* or *Malchut Shamayim*. 'The Day of the Lord' is the era when 'The Lord shall be king over all the earth: in that day shall the Lord be One and His Name One' (Zech. XIV: 9).

There are some references in Rabbinic literature to the 'banquet,' 'the huge Leviathan' and the 'wine preserved since the six days of Creation,'[2] for the delectation of the righteous at the end of days. These allusions are of a purely symbolic nature. 'In the world to come,' declares the Talmud, 'there is no eating – or drinking, nor procreation – or commerce, nor jealousy, enmity – or rivalry, but the righteous sit with crowns on their heads and enjoy the radiance of the Divine Presence.'[3]

Maimonides is even more explicit. 'In that (Messianic) era there shall be neither famine nor war, neither jealousy nor strife. Blessings will be abundant, comforts within the reach of all. The one preoccupation of the whole world will be to know the Lord ... as it is written: "For the earth shall be full of the knowledge of the Lord, as the waters cover the sea" ' (Isaiah XI: 9).[4]

OLAM HABA

Olam Haba, 'The world to come' and '*Leatid Lavo*' (the future that is to be) are terms that need clarification. 'In the

[1] *The Wisdom of Solomon* III: 1-4.
[2] *Baba Batra* 75a.
[3] *Berachot* 17a.
[4] *Yad Ha-Chazakah, Hilchot Melachim*, XII: 5.

eschatological doctrine of the Talmud a clear divergence of opinion may be traced. The earlier generations of the Rabbis identified the Messianic era with the World to Come. The promised Redeemer would bring the existing world-order to an end and inaugurate the timeless sphere in which the righteous would lead a purely spiritual existence freed from the trammels of the flesh. Subsequent teachers regarded the Messianic period as but a transitory stage between this world and the next.'[1]

Maimonides explains: 'The wise men called it "World to Come" not because it is not in existence at present, but because life in that world will come to man after the life in this world is ended.' In the words of the late Dr I. Epstein,[2] 'The World to Come, Olam Haba, has a twofold connotation, individual and universal. On the one hand, it denotes the heavenly world we each, individually, enter at death; on the other hand, it stands for the world in which the universality of mankind will enter upon its over-earthly destiny. The former is the sphere of Judgment and reward for our individual selves; the latter is the sphere of Resurrection and Judgment for all created beings. These two worlds are not distinct but represent two phases of the same process of fulfilment, the Olam Haba awaiting the individual at death having its consummation in the Olam Haba which follows the Resurrection.'

RESURRECTION

The Prophets spoke eloquently of the Resurrection. 'Thy dead shall live,' declared Isaiah. This belief in the resurrection of the dead is a fundamental principle of Judaism. 'And he who does not believe in it, is not an adherent of Judaism,' declared Maimonides,[3] the greatest rational Jewish philosopher of the Middle Ages.

[1] A. Cohen, op. cit. p. 386.
[2] The Faith of Judaism, p. 323.
[3] Commentary to Mishnah Sanhedrin x.1.

BODILY RESURRECTION

In the Second Benediction of the *Shemoneh Esreh* (the *Amidah*)[1] the resurrection is stressed and God is praised because 'Thou keepest Thy faith to them that sleep in the dust.'[2] The belief in the bodily resurrection was firmly held by Saadia Gaon (892–942),[3] Rashi[4] (1040–1105) and Rabbi Obadiah di Bertinoro (c. 1450–c. 1510).[5] Even the Sibylline Oracle (IV: 18) says: 'The dead rise with the bodies in which they died in order that they may be recognised,' while the *Talmud*[6] declares, 'They would be apparelled in their own clothes.'

The decomposition of the body did not present any difficulty to the Sages of the *Talmud* and *Midrash*[7] because resurrection was to be a purely miraculous act of God and for God nothing was too difficult.

TIME OF THE RESURRECTION

The resurrection will take place in the days of the Messiah. Elijah, who precedes the Messiah,[8] will herald the advent of the long-awaited Redeemer. 'Three days before the Messiah comes,' foretells the *Midrash*, 'Elijah will appear. On the first day, he will announce, "Peace has come to the world." On the second day he will announce, "Good has come to the world." On the third day, "Salvation has come to the world." The Holy One Blessed be He will make manifest His Glory, redeem Israel and the Era of Peace will begin.'[9]

[1] A.P.B. p. 95.   [2] *Ibid*, p. 47.
[3] *Emunot Ve-Deot*, VII: 7–9.   [4] Commentary on *Sanhedrin* 92a.
[5] Commentary on *Mishnah Sanhedrin* x.1.
[6] *Ketubot* 111b.
[7] Leviticus *Rabbah* xVIII.1, 'Hadrian asked Rabbi Joshua ben Chananiah: "From which part of the body will the Holy One Blessed be He, in time to come, cause man to sprout forth?" He answered: "From the nut of the spinal column." '
[8] Mal. III.23: 'The Resurrection of the dead will come through Elijah' (*Sotah* IX: 15).
[9] *Pesikta Rabbati* ed. M. Friedmann (Vienna, 1880) xxxv: 4, p. 161.

TRANSMIGRATION OF SOULS

Gilgul, the transmigration of the soul (Metempsychosis) is part of the teachings of the Cabbalah. 'Truly, all souls,' says the *Zohar*,[1] 'must undergo transmigration; but men do not perceive the ways of the Holy One, how the revolving scale is set up and men are judged every day at all times, and how they are brought before the Tribunal, both before they enter into this world and after they leave it. They perceive not the many transmigrations and the many mysterious works which the Holy One accomplishes with many naked souls, and how many naked spirits roam about in the other world without being able to enter within the veil of the King's Palace.'

The Cabbalistic school of Rabbi Isaac ben Solomon Ashkenazi Luria (1534–1572) and his disciple Rabbi Chayyim Vital believed that a soul that had sinned returned to its earthly existence in order to make amends. It was due to these mystical concepts of the impregnation (*Ibbur*) of souls[2] that the idea of *Dibbukim*[3] and *Gilgulim*[4] arose in mediaeval times.

Saadia Gaon,[5] Chasdai ben Abraham Crescas[6] (1340–1410) and Joseph Albo[7] (1380–1435) were sceptical of this belief.

SPIRITUALISM

It is forbidden for Jews to attempt to communicate with the dead.[8] Maimonides says[9] 'What is an *Ov*?[10] Standing

---

[1] *Zohar* III, 99*b* (*Mishpatim*).

[2] *Sepher Ha-Gilgulim* (The Book of Transmigration of Souls).

[3] *Dibbuk*—the soul of a sinner which attaches itself to a living body.

[4] *Gilgul*—Transmigration of a soul.

[5] *Emunot Vedeot* VI.

[6] *Or Adonai* IV: 7.

[7] *Ikkarim* IV: 29.

[8] Lev. XIX: 31; XX: 6. Deut. XVIII: 11.

[9] *Hilchot Avodah Zarah* VI: 1–2; Cf. A. E. Silverstone, *The Great Beyond*, p. 23.

[10] A necromancer or a wizard. From Isa. VIII: 19 it would appear that an *Ov* was a kind of ventriloquist who impersonated the dead.

and burning a known incense, holding a myrtle rod . . . or taking the skull of a dead person and burning incense to it. What is the *Yiddoni*? Placing a bone from the bird *Yiddon* in his mouth and burning incense . . . and all these are forms of idolatry. What is an "enquirer of the dead?" He who starves himself and sleeps in the cemetery so that a dead person may appear to him in a dream.'

The incident of Saul and the Witch of En Dor (I Sam. xxvIII: 7–19), the esoteric experiences of a number of Talmudic sages,[1] are isolated instances. Judaism believes implicitly in the existence of the spirit but rigorously opposes spiritualism, the attempt to contact these spirits. The dead should not be disturbed. Hence such practices are regarded as evil and undesirable and no better than idolatry and necromancy.

DIVINE GLORY

'The Rabbis,' writes the late Professor Louis Ginzberg (1873–1953)[2] 'often speak of the reward awaiting the righteous after their death as consisting not in material pleasure but in enjoying divine glory. Nevertheless, the development of the religious thought of the Jew shows a marked tendency to fix the centre of gravity of religion not in the thought of a world beyond but rather to fasten and establish it in the actual life of man on earth. In this respect the Scribes and the Rabbis were the true successors of the Prophets.'

[1] *Berachot* 18*b*; *Gittin* 56*b* and 57*a*; *Shabbat* 152*b*; Genesis *Rabbah* 100.7.
[2] *Students, Scholars and Saints*, pp. 97–8.

CHAPTER

XII

WORDS OF COMFORT

PSALM XVI

THIS Psalm gives us an insight into the quiet faith of an Israelite who has lived long in communion with God. He desires nothing else in life or death but the fellowship of God. In peril because impious enemies are closing in about him, the Psalmist appeals to God for help. His enemies are worldly men, seeking only this life's enjoyment. He, on the contrary, desires something far more satisfying—the beholding of God's majesty. Death cannot touch the heritage of the man whose heritage is the Lord.

Michtam of David. Keep me, O God; for I have taken refuge in Thee.
I have said unto the Lord: 'Thou art my Lord; I have no good but in Thee';
As for the holy that are in the earth,
They are the excellent in whom is all my delight.
Let the idols of them be multiplied that make suit unto another;
Their drink-offerings of blood will I not offer,
Nor take their names upon my lips.
O Lord, the portion of mine inheritance and of my cup,
Thou maintainest my lot.
The lines are fallen unto me in pleasant places;
Yea, I have a goodly heritage.
I will bless the Lord, who hath given me counsel;
Yea, in the night seasons my reins instruct me.

I have set the Lord always before me;
Surely He is at my right hand, I shall not be moved.
Therefore my heart is glad, and my glory rejoiceth;
My flesh also dwelleth in safety;
For Thou wilt not abandon my soul to the nether-world;
Neither wilt Thou suffer Thy godly one to see the pit.
Thou makest me to know the path of life;
In Thy presence is fulness of joy,
At Thy right hand bliss for evermore.

(Ps. xvi)

PSALM XXIII

This Psalm is one of the most beautiful and best loved in the entire Psalter. The Psalm breathes throughout a spirit of the calmest and most assured trust in God's providence: it speaks of a peace so deep, a serenity so profound, that even the thought of the shadow of death cannot trouble it. The Psalmist finds security not in a life of freedom from all dangers but in a life spent under God's direction and care. The picture is that of the shepherd leading his sheep through the narrow and dark gorges where unknown terror may lie in wait. But the shepherd is with them all the time and his presence is their strength and support.

A Psalm of David.
The Lord is my shepherd; I shall not want.
He maketh me to lie down in green pastures;
He leadeth me beside the still waters.
He restoreth my soul;
He guideth me in straight paths for His name's sake.
Yea, though I walk through the valley of the shadow of death,
I will fear no evil,
For Thou art with me;
Thy rod and Thy staff, they comfort me.
Thou preparest a table before me in the presence of mine enemies;

Thou hast anointed my head with oil; my cup runneth over.
Surely goodness and mercy shall follow me all the days of
 my life;
And I shall dwell in the house of the Lord for ever.

(Ps. xxiii)

PSALM XXXIX

Though provoked by the presence of the wicked who are
unpunished and rich, the Psalmist keeps his silence. With
wicked men, the Psalmist will not discuss his physical and
mental sufferings. Prolonged sickness has brought him to
the very edge of the grave. He will rather address himself
to God, to learn something about the brevity and emptiness
of human existence. In the eternity of God, man is but a
very fleeting figure and the ungodly rich are but a passing
shadow. His hope is in God alone from whom he asks
forgiveness for all his sins.

'Lord, make me to know mine end,
And the measure of my days, what it is:
Let me know how short-lived I am.
Behold, Thou hast made my days as hand-breadths;
And mine age is as nothing before Thee;
Surely every man at his best estate is altogether vanity.
 Selah.
Surely, man walketh as a mere semblance;
Surely for vanity they are in turmoil;
He heapeth up riches, and knoweth not who shall gather
 them.
And now, Lord, what wait I for?
My hope, it is in Thee.
Deliver me from all my transgressions;
Make me not the reproach of the base.
I was dumb, I open not my mouth;
Because Thou hast done it.
Remove Thy stroke from off me;
I am consumed by the blow of Thy Hand.

With rebukes dost Thou chasten man for iniquity.
And like a moth Thou makest his beauty to consume away;
Surely every man is vanity. Selah.
Hear my prayer, O Lord and give ear unto my cry;
Keep not silence at my tears;
For I am a stranger with Thee
A sojourner, as all my fathers were.
Look away from me, that I may take comfort,
Before I go hence, and be no more.'

(Ps. xxxix: 5-14)

PSALM XLIX

This Psalm deals with the problem: why are the ungodly rich and powerful and the faithful poor and oppressed? In one way or another this problem constantly reappears in the Bible. Faced with the terrible ordeal of suffering man is prone to doubt the goodness of the God whom he serves. The Psalmist resolves the problem by noting that all the wealth in the world cannot purchase exemption from death and it must all be abandoned when its owner comes to die. The Psalmist expresses his own faith that righteousness will be finally triumphant.

For the Leader: A Psalm of the sons of Korah.
Hear this, all ye peoples;
Give ear, all ye inhabitants of the world.
Both low and high,
Rich and poor together.
My mouth shall speak wisdom,
And the meditation of my heart shall be understanding.
I will incline mine ear to a parable;
I will open my dark saying upon the harp.
Wherefore should I fear in the days of evil,
When the iniquity of my supplanters compasseth me about.
Of them that trust in their wealth,
And boast themselves in the multitude of their riches?
No man can by any means redeem his brother,

Nor give to God a ransom for him—
For too costly is the redemption of their soul,
And must be let alone for ever—
That he should still live alway,
That he should not see the pit.
For he seeth that wise men die,
The fool and the brutish together perish,
And leave their wealth to others.
Their inward thought is, that their houses shall continue
    for ever,
And their dwelling-places to all generations;
They call their lands after their own names.
But man abideth not in honour;
He is like the beasts that perish.
This is the way of them that are foolish,
And of those who after them approve their sayings. Selah.
Like sheep they are appointed for the nether-world;
Death shall be their shepherd;
And the upright shall have dominion over them in the
    morning;
And their form shall be for the nether-world to wear away,
That there be no habitation for it.
But God will redeem my soul from the power of the
    nether-world;
For He shall receive me. Selah.
Be not thou afraid when one waxeth rich,
When the wealth of his house is increased;
For when he dieth he shall carry nothing away;
His wealth shall not descend after him.
Though while he lived he blessed his soul:
'Men will praise thee, when thou shalt do well to thyself:'
It shall go to the generation of his fathers;
They shall never see the light.
Man that is in honour understandeth not;
He is like the beasts that perish.

(Ps. XLIX)

PSALM CIII

The Psalmist summons his soul and all his faculties to praise God for pardon, redemption and bountiful provision for every need. Man may be frail and transitory but those who fear God can rest in the assurance of his eternal faithfulness. Man is mortal and frail but God's mercy is eternal.

As for man, his days are as grass;
As a flower of the field, so he flourisheth.
For the wind passeth over it, and it is gone;
And the place thereof knoweth it no more.
But the mercy of the Lord is from everlasting to everlasting
  upon them that fear Him,
And His righteousness unto children's children.

(Ps. CIII: 15–18)

PROVERBS XXXI

This is a beautiful acrostic poem, the first verse beginning with the first letter of the Hebrew alphabet and each of the remaining twenty-one letters coming in turn. It is an ode to the perfect wife, the ideal housewife. It shows the elevated social position of woman among the Hebrews as compared with that which she held among other ancient nations. The good wife is more precious than jewels. Her kingdom is the home. The poem shows how happiness in the domestic circle depends upon the foresight of this queen of the hearth.

THE WOMAN OF VIRTUE

A woman of valour who can find?
For her price is far above rubies.
The heart of her husband doth safely trust in her,
And he hath no lack of gain.
She doeth him good and not evil
All the days of her life.
She seeketh wool and flax,
And worketh willingly with her hands.
She is like the merchant-ships;

138

She bringeth her food from afar.
She riseth also while it is yet night,
And giveth food to her household,
And a portion to her maidens.
She considereth a field, and buyeth it;
With the fruit of her hands she planteth a vineyard.
She girdeth her loins with strength,
And maketh strong her arms.
She perceiveth that her merchandise is good;
Her lamp goeth not out by night.
She layeth her hands to the distaff,
And her hands hold the spindle.
She stretcheth out her hand to the poor;
Yea, she reacheth forth her hands to the needy.
She is not afraid of the snow for her household;
For all her household are clothed with scarlet.
She maketh for herself coverlets;
Her clothing is fine linen and purple.
Her husband is known in the gates,
When he sitteth among the elders of the land.
She maketh linen garments and selleth them;
And delivereth girdles unto the merchant.
Strength and dignity are her clothing;
And she laugheth at the time to come.
She openeth her mouth with wisdom;
And the law of kindness is on her tongue.
She looketh well to the ways of her household,
And eateth not the bread of idleness.
Her children rise up, and call her blessed;
Her husband also, and he praiseth her:
'Many daughters have done valiantly,
But thou excellest them all.'
Grace is deceitful, and beauty is vain;
But a woman that feareth the Lord, she shall be praised.
Give her of the fruit of her hands;
And let her works praise her in the gates.

(PROVERBS XXXI: 10–31)

The Book of Job wrestles with the problem of the meaning of sorrow. Job was a wealthy man living a semi-nomadic life, free from worldly cares, when suddenly catastrophe struck and he was faced with the problem of human suffering. Satan is portrayed as asserting that Job serves God only because it is profitable. God accepts the challenge and Satan is allowed to afflict Job in order to prove that the good man does not serve God merely because it pays him well to do so. Contrary to Satan's predictions, Job does not curse God in his misfortunes but blesses him. He believed that God effectively and at every moment controls the world and human life. The book was written for the purpose of seeking an answer to questions concerning the reason for human suffering and why a loving God allows it.

Then Job arose, and rent his mantle, and shaved his head, and
    fell down upon the ground, and worshipped; and he said:
Naked came I out of my mother's womb,
And naked shall I return thither;
The Lord gave, and the Lord hath taken away;
Blessed be the name of the Lord.
For all this Job sinned not, nor ascribed aught unseemly to
    God.   (JOB I: 20–22)

ECCLESIASTES

Ecclesiastes presents some practical considerations designed to alleviate misery and suggests that sorrow and even death are blessings and that patience and wisdom will enable man not only to bear but even to profit by inevitable misfortunes. He who would live wisely must lay death at heart and integrate it.

A good name is better than precious oil;
And the day of death than the day of one's birth.
It is better to go to the house of mourning,
Than to go to the house of feasting;
For that is the end of all men,
And the living will lay it to his heart.

                        (ECCLESIASTES VII: 1–2)

Man is a creature of time. Ecclesiastes recommends the frank recognition of our creaturelessness even in youth when life seems unquenchable. He is viewing the dissolution of the body and spirit and he simply states that each returns to the source from which it sprang, the body to the dust and the spirit to God. The passage describes the failings of an old man's physical powers. The Talmud (*Shabbat* 152a) explained the 'sun' as forehead, 'Light' as nose, 'moon' as soul and 'stars' as cheeks.

Remember then thy Creator in the days of thy youth,
Before the evil days come,
And the years draw nigh, when thou shalt say:
'I have no pleasure in them';
Before the sun, and light, and the moon,
And the stars, are darkened,
And the clouds return after the rain;

(ECCLESIASTES XII: 1–2)

And the dust returneth to the earth as it was,
And the spirit returneth unto God who gave it.

(*Ibid.*, v. 7)

The end of the matter, all having been heard: fear God, and
keep His commandments; for this is the whole man.

(*Ibid.*, 13)

THE RIGHTEOUS CANNOT DIE

'But the souls of the righteous are in the hand of God,
And no torment shall touch them.
In the eyes of the foolish they seemed to have died;
And their departure was accounted to be to their hurt,
And their journeying away from us to be their ruin:
But they are in peace.
For even if in the sight of men they be punished,
Their hope is full of immortality:
And having borne a little chastening, they shall receive
great good;

141

Because God made trial of them and found them worthy of himself.'

(THE WISDOM OF SOLOMON III: 1–6)

The Wisdom of Solomon, one of the books of the *Apocrypha* was probably written by an Alexandrian Jew who lived between 100 B.C.E. and 50 C.E.

'Rabbi[1] Tarfon said, The day is short, and the work is great, and the labourers are sluggish, and the reward is much, and the Master is urgent. He used also to say, It is not thy duty to complete the work, but neither art thou free to desist from it; if thou hast studied much Torah, much reward will be given thee; and faithful is thy Employer to pay thee the reward of thy labour; and know that the grant of reward unto the righteous will be in the time to come.'

(Abot II: 20–21)

'Rabbi[2] Jacob said: This world is like a vestibule before the world to come; prepare thyself in the vestibule, that thou mayest enter into the hall. He used to say, "Better is one hour of repentance and good deeds in this world than the whole life of the world to come; and better is one hour of blissfulness of spirit in the world to come than the whole life of this world".'

(Abot IV: 21)

'Rabbi[3] Jose, the son of Kisma, said, I was once walking by the way, when a man met me and greeted me, and I returned his greeting. He said to me, Rabbi, from what place art thou? I said to him, I come from a great city of sages and scribes. He said to me, if thou art willing to dwell with us in our place, I will give thee a thousand thousand golden dinars and precious stones and pearls. I said to him,

[1] He flourished towards the end of the first and the beginning of the second centuries.

[2] Rabbi Jacob ben Korshai flourished towards the end of the second century.

[3] He flourished at the beginning of the second century.

Wert thou to give me all the silver and gold and precious stones and pearls in the world I would not dwell anywhere but in a home of the Torah; and thus it is written in the Book of Psalms by the hands of David King of Israel, The law of thy mouth is better unto me than thousands of gold and silver; and not only so, but in the hour of man's departure neither silver nor gold nor precious stones nor pearls accompany him, but only Torah and good works, as it is said, When thou walkest it shall lead thee; when thou liest down it shall watch over thee; and when thou awakest it shall talk with thee:—when thou walkest it shall lead thee—in this world; when thou liest down it shall watch over thee—in the grave; and when thou awakest it shall talk with thee—in the world to come. And it says, The silver is mine, and the gold is mine, saith the Lord of hosts.'

(Abot vi: 9)

Rabbi Meir said: Whence do we learn that as you should say a blessing over the good, so you should say a blessing over the evil? Because it says, 'Which the Lord thy God gives thee' (DEUT. viii: 10). And 'thy God' means 'thy judge'; in every judgment with which He judges you, whether with the attribute of good or with the attribute of punishment, bless God.

(Berachot 48b)

When Rabbi[1] Jochanan finished the Book of Job he used to say the following: The end of man is to die, and the end of a beast is to be slaughtered, and all are doomed to die. Happy is he who was brought up in the Torah and whose labour was in the Torah and who has given pleasure to his Creator and who grew up with a good name and departed the world with a good name; and of him Solomon said: A good name is better than precious oil, and the day of death than the day of one's birth (ECCL. viii: 1).

(Berachot 17a)

[1] Rabbi Jochanan ben Nappacha 190–279 was head of the Academy at Tiberias.

When Rabban[1] Jochanan ben Zakkai fell ill, his disciples
went in to visit him. When he saw them he began to weep.
His disciples said to him: Lamp of Israel, pillar of the right
hand, mighty hammer! Wherefore weepest thou? He replied
if I were being taken today before a human king who is here
today and tomorrow in the grave, whose anger if he is angry
with one does not last for ever, who if he imprisons me does
not imprison me for ever and who if he puts me to death
does not put me to everlasting death, and whom I can
persuade with words and bribe with money, even so I
would weep. Now that I am being taken before the
supreme King of Kings, the Holy One, blessed be He, who
lives and endures for ever and ever, whose anger, if He is
angry with me, is an everlasting anger, who if he imprisons
me imprisons me for ever, who if He puts me to death puts
me to death for ever, and whom I cannot persuade with
words or bribe with money—nay more, when there are
two ways before me, one leading to Paradise and the other
to Gehinnom, and I do not know by which I shall be taken,
shall I not weep?

(Berachot 28b)

It once came to pass that Hillel[2] the elder was coming
from a journey, and he heard a great cry in the city, and
he said: I am confident that this does not come from my
house. Of him Scripture says: He shall not be afraid of the
evil tidings; his heart is steadfast trusting in the Lord (Ps.
cxii: 7).

(Berachot 60a)

Raba[3] said, When man is led in for judgment (in the
next world) he is asked: Did you deal faithfully, did you
fix times for learning, did you engage in procreation, did
you hope for salvation . . . Yet even so, if 'the fear of the

[1] He flourished during the first century and belonged to the
first generation of Tannaim.
[2] He lived from 30 B.C.E. to 10 C.E.
[3] A leading Amora of the third generation (270–330)

Lord is his treasure' (Is. XXXIII: 6) it will go well with him: if not, it will not.

(Shabbat 31a)

Rabbi Simeon b. Pazzi said in the name of Rabbi Joshua b. Levi in Bar Kappara's name: if one sheds tears for a worthy man, the Holy One, blessed be He, counts them and lays them up in His treasure house, for it is said: Thou countest my grievings: Put thou my tears into thy bottle; Are they not in thy book? (Ps. LVI: 9).

(Shabbath 105b)

'Blessed shalt thou be when thou comest in, and blessed shalt thou be when thou goest out' (DEUT. XXVIII: 3)—that thine exit from the world shall be as thine entry therein: just as thou enterest it without sin, so mayest thou leave it without.

(Baba Mezia 107a)

Rabbi Simlai said: Six hundred and thirteen commandments were given to Moses, 365 negative commandments, answering to the number of the days of the year, and 248 positive commandments, answering to the number of the members of man's body. Then David came and reduced them to eleven (eleven commands are found in Psalm xv). Then came Isaiah, and reduced them to six. Then came Micah, and reduced them to three (as is seen in the great saying of Micah VI: 8). Then Isaiah came again, and reduced them to two, as it is said, 'Keep ye justice and do righteousness'. Then came Amos, and reduced them to one, as it is said, 'Seek ye me and live'. Or one may say, then came Habakkuk (II: 4) and reduced them to one, as it is said, 'The righteous shall live by his faith'.

(Makkot 23b–24a)

Rabbi Jochanan said: if a man's first wife dies, it is as if the Temple were destroyed in his day. Rabbi Alexandri said: if a man's wife dies the world becomes dark for him.

Rabbi Samuel ben Nachman said: For everything there is a substitute except for the wife of one's youth.

(*Sanhedrin* 22*a*)

A king had a vineyard in which he employed many laborers, one of whom demonstrated special aptitude and skill. What did the king do? He took this laborer from his work and strolled through the garden conversing with him. When the laborers came for their wages in the evening, the skilful laborer also appeared among them and he received a full day's wages from the king. The other laborers were angry at this and protested. 'We had labored the whole day while this man has worked but two hours; why does the king give him the full wage, even as to us?' The king said to them: 'Why are you angry? Through his skill he has done in two hours more than you have done all day.' So it is with Rabbi Abin[1] ben Hiyya. In the twenty-eight years of his life he has attained more in Torah than others in a hundred years.

(*Yerushalmi Berachot* ii: 8. Ecc. *Rabbah* vi)

'And God saw everything which He had made, and behold it was very good' (Gen. i: 31). Why does death befall the righteous and not only the wicked? It had to befall the righteous too, or else the wicked might have said, 'The righteous live because they practise the Law and good works: we will do so too,' and they would have fulfilled the commandments deceitfully, and not for their own sake. Again, death befalls the wicked, because they cause vexation to God. But when they die, they cease to vex Him. Death befalls the righteous, because all their life they have to struggle with their evil inclination; when they die, they are at peace.'

(*Genesis Rabbah* ix: 5–9)

Two ships were once seen to be sailing near land. One of them was going forth from the harbor, and the other

[1] Rabbi Zera in a funeral oration at the untimely death of Rabbi Abin at the age of 28.

was coming into the harbor. Every one was cheering the outgoing ship, every one was giving it a hearty send off. But the incoming ship was scarcely noticed.

A wise man was looking at the two ships, and he said: 'I see here a paradox; for surely, people should not rejoice at the ship leaving the harbor, since they know not what destiny awaits it, what storms it may encounter, what dangers it may have to undergo. Rejoice rather over the ship that has reached port safely and brought back all its passengers in peace.'

It is the way of the world that when a human being is born, all rejoice; but when he dies, all sorrow. Rather ought the opposite to be the case. No one can tell what troubles await the child on its journey into manhood. But when a man has lived and dies in peace, all should rejoice, seeing that he has completed his journey, and is departing this world with the imperishable crown of a good name.

(*Ex. Rabba Va-Yakhel* XLVIII: 1–2)

THE FOX AND THE GRAPES

A hungry fox was eyeing some luscious fruit in a garden, but to his dismay, he could find no way to enter. At last he discovered an opening through which, he thought, he might possibly get in, but he soon found that the hole was too small to admit his body. 'Well,' he thought, 'if I fast three days I will be able to squeeze through.' He did so; and he now feasted to his heart's delight on the grapes and all the other good things in the orchard. But when he wanted to escape, he discovered that the opening had again become too small for him. Again he had to fast three days and as he escaped he said: 'O garden, what have I now for all my labor and cunning?'

So it is with man. Naked he comes into the world, naked must he leave it. After all his labor he carries nothing away with him except the good deeds he leaves behind.

(*Midrash, Ecclesiastes Rabbah* 5: 1)

'Not merely should we be ready to receive the evil as well as the good from God, but a man should rejoice over sufferings more than over good, for if a man is in prosperity all his life, his sins will not be forgiven him. But they are forgiven him through sufferings. Rabbi Eliezer b. Jacob quoted the verse, Proverbs III: 12, "Whom God loves He chastens, even as the father chastens the son of whom he is fond." What causes the son to be loved by his father? Sufferings. Rabbi Meir quoted the verse, Deuteronomy VIII: 5 "As a father chastens his son, so God has chastened thee." God says, "Thou, Israel, knowest the deeds which thou hast done, and that the sufferings which I have brought upon thee are not in proportion to thy deeds." Rabbi Jose b. Judah said: Beloved are sufferings before God, for the glory of God rests upon sufferers.'

(Sifre. Deut. *Va'etchanan,* 32)

Rabbi Simeon ben Yochai[1] says: Chastisements are precious; for the Holy One blessed be He, gave three gifts to Israel which the nations of the world desire, and he gave them to Israel only through chastisements. They are: the Torah, and the land of Israel, and the world to come. Whence do we know this of the Torah? For it is written: 'Happy is the man whom thou chastenest, O Lord, and teachest him out of thy Torah (Ps. XC: 12). Whence do we know this of the land of Israel? For it is written: 'So the Lord thy God chasteneth thee' (Deut. XVIII: 5) and afterwards: 'The Lord thy God bringeth thee into a good land, a land of brooks of water, of fountains and depths, springing forth in valleys and hills.' Whence do we know this of the world to come? For it is written: 'For the commandment is a lamp, and the teaching is light, and reproofs of instruction are the way of life' (Prov. VI: 23). Which is the way that brings a man to the world to come? It is chastisement.

(Sifra on Deut. XXXVI: 5 ed. Friedmann, 73*b*)

[1] He lived ca. 130–160 and was a disciple of Rabbi Akiba.

When Aaron heard of the death of his two sons, he 'held his peace' (Lev. x: 3); he acknowledged the justice of the divine decree. With the righteous it is habitual to act thus. So did Abraham, when he said, 'I am but dust and ashes' (Gen. XVIII: 27); so did Jacob and David.

(*Sifra* ed. I. H. Weiss and J. Schlossberg, Vienna, 1862, 45*a*)

Rabbi Meir[1] sat discoursing on a Sabbath afternoon in the House of Study. While he was there, his two sons died. What did their mother[2] do? She laid them upon the bed, and spread a linen cloth over them. At the outgoing of the Sabbath Rabbi Meir came home and said to her, 'Where are my sons?' She replied, 'They went to the House of Study.' He said, 'I did not see them there.' She gave him the Havdalah cup, and he said again, 'Where are my sons?' She said, 'They went to another place, and now they have returned.' She gave him to eat and he ate and recited the blessing. Then she said, 'I have a question to ask you.' He replied, 'Ask it.' She said, 'Early today a man came here, and gave me something to keep for him; now he has come back to ask for it again. Shall we return it to him or not?' He replied, 'He who has received something on deposit must surely return it to its owner.' She replied, 'Without your knowledge I would not return it.' Then she took him by the hand, and brought him up to the bed, and took away the cloth, and he saw his sons lying dead upon the bed. Then he began to weep, and said about each, 'O my son, my son; O my Rabbi, my Rabbi! My sons, as all men would say; Rabbi, Rabbi because they gave light to their father's face through their knowledge of the Law.' Then his wife said to him, 'Did you not say to me that one must return a deposit to its owner? Does it not say, "The Lord gave, the Lord took, blessed be the name of the Lord"?' (Job I: 21). Thus she comforted him and quietened his mind.

(*Midrash* on Proverbs XXXI: 10)

[1] He flourished during the second century and was a disciple of Rabbi Akiba.

[2] Beruryah wife of R. Meir.

'Teach us to number our days' (Ps. xc: 12). Rabbi Joshua said: 'If we know for certain the exact number of days in our lives we would repent before we died.' Rabbi Eleazar taught: 'Repent one day before thy death.' When his disciples asked: 'Is there a man who knows when he will die?' he replied: 'All the more reason for a man to repent today, lest he die tomorrow. Thus all the days of his life will be spent in penitence.'

(The *Midrash* on Psalms cx: 16 ed. William G. Braude (New Haven, 1959) Vol. ii, p. 97.)

A man has three friends: His children and household, his wealth and his good deeds. When about to depart from this world, he appeals to his children: 'Save me.' They say to him: 'There is no man that hath power over the day of death' (Eccl. viii: 8); 'No man can by any means redeem his brother' (Ps. xlix: 8). His wealth replies to him: 'Riches profit not in the day of wrath' (Prov. xi: 4). But his good deeds say to him: 'Before you come for judgment, we shall be there ahead of you:' as it is written (Is. lviii: 8): 'And thy righteousness shall go before thee, the glory of the Lord shall be thy reward.'

(*Pirke D'rabbi Eliezer*, Chap. xxxiv: *Yalkut Shimoni*, Is. 58, 494)

It is related that an ass-driver came to Rabbi Akiba and said to him, 'Rabbi, teach me the whole Torah all at once.' He replied, 'My son, Moses our teacher stayed on the Mount forty days and forty nights before he learned it, and you want me to teach you the whole of it at once! Still, my son, this is the basic principle of the Torah: What is hateful to yourself, do not to your fellow-man. If you wish nobody should harm you in connection with what belongs to you, you must not harm him in that way; if you wish that nobody should take away from you what is yours, do not take away from another what is his.' The man rejoined his companions, and thy journeyed until they came to a field full of seed-pods. His companions each took two, but he took none.

They continued their journey, and came to a field full of cabbages. They each took two, but he took none. They asked him why he had not taken any, and he replied, 'Thus did Rabbi Akiba teach me: What is hateful to yourself, do not to your fellow-man. If you wish that nobody should take from you what is yours, do not take from another what is his.'

(*Abot de Rabbi Nathan*, ed. S. Schechter, London, 1887 XXVI, f. 27*a*)

With regard to the great bliss which the soul is to attain in the world to come—there is no possibility of comprehending or of knowing it whilst we are in this world; seeing that here beneath we are sensible of that only which is good for the body. But with respect to the celestial bliss, it is so exceedingly great, that all earthly good can bear no comparison with it, except by way of figure. So that truly to estimate the happiness of the soul in the world to come by the happiness of the body in this world, as for instance in eating or drinking, is utterly impossible. This is what David meant in exclaiming, 'Oh how abundant is Thy goodness, which Thou hast laid up for them that fear Thee' (Ps. XXXI: 20).

(The *Mishneh Torah* by Moses Maimonides (1135–1204), Book of Knowledge, Section on 'Repentance', VIII: 6.)

O my God, the soul which thou gavest me is pure; thou didst create it, thou didst form it, thou didst breathe it into me. Thou preservest it within me, and thou wilt take it from me, but wilt restore it unto me hereafter. So long as the soul is within me, I will give thanks unto thee, O Lord my God and God of my fathers, Sovereign of all works, Lord of all souls! Blessed art thou, O Lord, who restorest souls unto the dead.

(From the morning Service)

Since my brother is gone my world is no more wide; it is a prison, and the earth is like shackles. He that upheld the glory of all things, how is it that his back is now burdened with dust? Because he is gone the sun is the companion of jackals, the moon is the brother of mourning since his death. Now shall all understand that heaven's host will fade and shrivel as a withering bud (all this shall vanish as a clod of earth, and yet the memory of his glory never shall grow old). When my brother went to the grave, I knew that all creation is but vanity.

(Ch. Brody, in Steinschneider's *Festschrift*, Leipzig (1896) p. 43)

Moses b. Jacob Ibn Ezra (1070–) Dirge on the Death of his brother

The soul is likened to the moon, and the sun is God, who is blessed, as it is written: 'The Lord God is a sun and a shield' (Ps. LXXXIV: 12). Now just as the moon, when it approaches the sun, its light becomes stronger above; even so the divine soul, when it draws nearer to God, who is blessed, and forsakes pleasures and worldly affairs, its light becomes fuller, and it attains bliss; for the way of life is upward to the wise. But when it removes itself from God, who is blessed, and clings to the affairs of the body, making God's service subordinate, it becomes dark on the upper part, and only sheds its light from its lower part upon bodily and worldly things. This is the cause of its perdition with regards to spiritual matters which occasion and bring about its welfare. It is on account of this circumstance that our teachers of blessed memory tell us that the preservation and light of the soul depend on its being turned towards God's countenance, and that its perdition and death are caused by its removing itself from Him; as it is written: 'Lo, they that go far from Thee shall perish' (*Ibid.*, LXXIII: 27).

(*Nishmat Chayyim* (Soul of Life), part 2, chapter 30)

Menasseh ben Israel (1604–1657)

An old Saxon chieftain on a wintry day was revelling with his warriors in the banqueting hall, when he noticed a sparrow fly in at one door, hover a moment over the light and warmth of the hearth-fire, fly across the hall to the other door, and vanish into the night whence it came. 'So seems the life of man,' he exclaimed. 'Out of the darkness we come, we enjoy for a while the warmth and sunshine of the world, and then again into darkness we lapse.' This is strikingly beautiful, but heathen, gloomy, false. Man's life is not a journey from darkness to darkness. There is within us a divine spark. We come from God, and we go back to God. 'The dust returneth to the earth as it was, but the spirit returneth unto God who gave it.' If we have lived justly, loved mercy and walked in humility with God and man, then the end of our toil is not a flight into darkness; but to that life which is wholly a Sabbath-rest with God, peace everlasting.

(The authorised Daily Prayer Book with a commentary by
Dr. J. H. Hertz, p. 1102)

Dr. Joseph Herman Hertz (1872–1946) was Chief Rabbi of the British Empire from 1913–1946. His publications include English commentaries on the Pentateuch and prayer-book.

WHO HAS LIVED?

'*And Jacob lived*' (Gen. XLVII: 28). Of how few men, asks a famous modern Jewish preacher, can we repeat a phrase like 'And Jacob *lived?*' When many a man dies, a death-notice appears in the Press. In reality, it is a life-notice; because but for it, the world would never have known that that man had ever been alive. Only he who has been a force for human goodness, and abides in hearts and souls made better by his presence during his pilgrimage on earth, can be said to have *lived*, only such a one is heir to immortality.

(Joseph H. Hertz, *The Pentateuch and Haftorahs*, p. 180)

A PLEDGE FROM THE LIVING

The father's heart beat no more. The kindly eye was closed forever . . . The son had stepped into the parent's

153

shoes. He had undertaken the responsibilities for the honor of his house. And there at the open grave . . . he stood in the presence of the whole congregation of friends and strangers and those who were to lead in the age after him, and there at the saddest moment of his life he recalled neither sorrow nor his loss, but his duty.   As a Jew he knew the holiness of the moment, and he framed his resolution in the words holiest to Jewish hearts; there he opened his lips and made a pledge, a holy promise: '*Yisgadal Veyisskadash Shmeh Rabba* Lord God, I do not murmur against Thy decree, I am a child of Jewry. Lord God, hear my voice at this moment. As my father lived for Thee, as his life was dedicated to Thy glory and Thy name, so do I declare *Yisgadal Veyisskadash* that Thy great Name may be magnified and sanctified 'as the promise for my future. So do I undertake to remember his fidelity, and never to forget my own duty.'

That was the meaning of Kaddish in the generations of our fathers. That is the meaning of the words today when said for mother and father. Not a prayer for the dead, but a pledge from the living; not a superstitious phrase, but a man's motto of life.

(Leo Jung, *Yisgadal We'yiskadash* (Union of Orthodox Jewish Congregation of America publication, pp. 6–7). (Rabbi Dr. Leo Jung, spiritual leader of the New York Jewish Center, is the author and editor of many standard works of Judaica.)

CHAPTER

XIII

MEMORIAL PRAYERS

CONTENTS:

Mourner's Kaddish, Hebrew, translation and transliteration in Ashkenazi and Sephardi pronunciation; the Scholar's Kaddish, Hebrew, translation and transliteration in Ashkenazi and Sephardi; the Burial Kaddish, Hebrew, translation and transliteration; Memorial prayer for father, Hebrew, translation and transliteration; prayer in memory of a mother, Hebrew, translation and transliteration; a memorial prayer for a husband, wife, daughter, sister, child; a prayer in memory of Jewish martyrs.

MOURNER'S KADDISH

Mourner—Magnified and sanctified be His great name in the world which He hath created according to His will. May He establish His kingdom during your life and during your days, and during the life of all the house of Israel, even speedily and at a near time, and say ye, Amen.

Congregation and Mourner—Let His great name be blessed for ever and to all eternity.

Mourner—Blessed, praised and glorified, exalted, extolled and honored, magnified and lauded be the name of the Holy One, blessed be He; though He be high above all the blessings and hymns, praises and consolations, which are uttered in the world; and say ye, Amen.

Mourner—May there be abundant peace from heaven, and life for us and for all Israel; and say ye, Amen.

Mourner—He who maketh peace in his high places, may He make peace for us and for all Israel; and say ye, Amen.

MOURNERS KADDISH קַדִּישׁ יָתוֹם

יִתְגַּדַּל וְיִתְקַדַּשׁ שְׁמֵהּ רַבָּא, בְּעָלְמָא דִי־בְרָא
כִרְעוּתֵהּ, וְיַמְלִיךְ מַלְכוּתֵהּ, בְּחַיֵּיכוֹן וּבְיוֹמֵיכוֹן, וּבְחַיֵּי
דְכָל־בֵּית יִשְׂרָאֵל, בַּעֲגָלָא וּבִזְמַן קָרִיב. וְאִמְרוּ אָמֵן.
Cong. אָמֵן

Cong. יְהֵא שְׁמֵהּ רַבָּא מְבָרַךְ לְעָלַם וּלְעָלְמֵי
עָלְמַיָּא.

יִתְבָּרַךְ וְיִשְׁתַּבַּח וְיִתְפָּאַר וְיִתְרוֹמַם וְיִתְנַשֵּׂא וְיִתְהַדָּר
וְיִתְעַלֶּה וְיִתְהַלָּל שְׁמֵהּ דְּקֻדְשָׁא. Cong. בְּרִיךְ הוּא
(During the Ten Days of Pentinence, add: לְעֵלָּא (וּלְעֵלָּא
מִן כָּל־בִּרְכָתָא, וְשִׁירָתָא תֻּשְׁבְּחָתָא, וְנֶחֱמָתָא
דַּאֲמִירָן בְּעָלְמָא. וְאִמְרוּ אָמֵן. Cong. אָמֵן

יְהֵא שְׁלָמָא רַבָּא מִן־שְׁמַיָּא וְחַיִּים עָלֵינוּ
וְעַל כָּל־יִשְׂרָאֵל. וְאִמְרוּ אָמֵן. Cong. אָמֵן

עוֹשֶׂה שָׁלוֹם בִּמְרוֹמָיו, הוּא יַעֲשֶׂה שָׁלוֹם
עָלֵינוּ. וְעַל כָּל־יִשְׂרָאֵל. וְאִמְרוּ אָמֵן. Cong. אָמֵן

TRANSLITERATION OF THE MOURNER'S KADDISH
Ashkenazi pronunciation

Yisgaddal v'yiskaddash sh'mey rabboh
B'olmoh dee-v'ro chir-usey,
V'yamlich malchusey
B'chay-yeychon uv'yo-meychon
'Uv'chay-yey de-chol beys yisro-eyl
Ba-agoloh uvizman koreev
V'imru omeyn.
Y'hey sh'mey rabboh m'vorach
L'olam ul'olmey olmah-yoh
Yisborach, v'yishtabach,
V'yispo-ar v'yisromam,
V'yisnassey v'yis-haddar
V'yis-alleh v'yis-hallal
Sh'mey de-kudshoh, b'reech hu
L'eyloh[1] min kol birchosoh v'shirosoh
Tush-b'chosoh v'nechemosoh
Daa-amiron b'olmoh
V'imru omeyn.
Y'hey sh'lomoh rabboh min sh'mah-yoh,
V'chay-im oleynu v'al kol yisro-eyl
V'imru omeyn.
O-seh sholom bimromov
Hu ya-aseh sholom
Oleynu v'al kol yisroe-eyl
V'imru omeyn.

[1] During the Ten Days of Penitence from Rosh Hashanah to Yom Kippur, repeat the word *L'eyloh*.

MOURNER'S KADDISH
Sephardi pronunciation

Yitgaddal v'yitkaddash sh'meh rabbah
B'almah dee-v'ra chiru-teh
V'yamlich malchuteh
B'chay-yechon uv'yo-meychon
Uv'chay-yey de-chol beit yisra-el
Ba-agalah uvizman kareev;
V'imru Amen.
Y'hey sh'mey rabbah m'varach
L'olam ul'olmey almah-yah.
Yitbarach v'yishtabach,
V'yitpa-ar v'yitromam
V'yitnasseh v'yit-haddar
V'yit-alleh v'yit-hallal
Sh'mey de kudshah b'reech hu
L'eylah min kol birchatah v'shiratah
Tush-b'chatah v'nechematah
Daa-amiran b'almah
V'imru Amen
Y'heh sh'lamah rabbah min sh'mayah
V'chay-yim alenu v'al kol yisra-el
V'imru Amen
O-seh shalom bimromav
Hu ya-aseh shalom
Alenu v'al kol yisra-el
V'imru Amen.

KADDISH D'RABBANAN

Reader—Magnified and sanctified be His great name in the world which He hath created according to His will. May He establish His kingdom during your life and during your days, and during the life of all the house of Israel, even speedily and at a near time, and say ye, Amen.

Congregation and Reader—Let His great name be blessed for ever and to all eternity.

Reader—Blessed, praised, and glorified, exalted, extolled and honored, magnified and lauded be the name of the Holy One, blessed be He; though He be high above all the blessings and hymns, praises and consolations, which are uttered in the world; and say ye, Amen.

Unto Israel, and unto the Rabbis, and unto their disciples, and unto all the disciples of their disciples, and unto all who engage in the study of the Law, in this or in any other place, unto them and unto you be abundant peace, grace, lovingkindness, mercy, long life, ample sustenance and salvation from the Father who is in heaven, and say ye, Amen.

Reader—May there be abundant peace from heaven, and a happy life for us and for all Israel; and say ye, Amen.

Reader—He who maketh peace in his high places, may He in his mercy make peace for us and for all Israel; and say ye, Amen.

יִתְגַּדַּל וְיִתְקַדַּשׁ שְׁמֵהּ רַבָּא, בְּעָלְמָא דִי־בְרָא

כִרְעוּתֵהּ, וְיַמְלִיךְ מַלְכוּתֵהּ, בְּחַיֵּיכוֹן וּבְיוֹמֵיכוֹן, וּבְחַיֵּי

דְכָל־בֵּית יִשְׂרָאֵל, בַּעֲגָלָא וּבִזְמַן קָרִיב. וְאִמְרוּ אָמֵן.

Cong. אָמֵן

יְהֵא שְׁמֵהּ רַבָּא מְבָרַךְ לְעָלַם וּלְעָלְמֵי .Cong

עָלְמַיָּא.

יִתְבָּרַךְ וְיִשְׁתַּבַּח וְיִתְפָּאַר וְיִתְרוֹמַם וְיִתְנַשֵּׂא וְיִתְהַדָּר

וְיִתְעַלֶּה וְיִתְהַלָּל שְׁמֵהּ דְּקֻדְשָׁא. Cong. בְּרִיךְ הוּא

(*During the Ten Days of Pentinence, add:* (וּלְעֵלָּא) לְעֵלָּא

מִן כָּל־בִּרְכָתָא, וְשִׁירָתָא תֻּשְׁבְּחָתָא, וְנֶחֱמָתָא

דַּאֲמִירָן בְּעָלְמָא. וְאִמְרוּ אָמֵן. Cong. אָמֵן

עַל יִשְׂרָאֵל וְעַל רַבָּנָן וְעַל תַּלְמִידֵיהוֹן וְעַל כָּל־

תַּלְמִידֵי תַלְמִידֵיהוֹן וְעַל כָּל־מָן דִּי עָסְקִין בְּאוֹרַיְתָא דִי

בְאַתְרָא הָדֵן וְדִי בְּכָל־אֲתַר וַאֲתַר יְהֵא לְהוֹן וּלְכוֹן

שְׁלָמָא רַבָּא חִנָּא וְחִסְדָּא וְרַחֲמִין וְחַיִּין אֲרִיכִין וּמְזוֹנָא

רְוִיחָא וּפָרְקָנָא מִן־קֳדָם אֲבוּהוֹן דִּי בִשְׁמַיָּא. וְאִמְרוּ

אָמֵן:

יְהֵא שְׁלָמָא רַבָּא מִן־שְׁמַיָּא וְחַיִּים עָלֵינוּ

וְעַל כָּל־יִשְׂרָאֵל. וְאִמְרוּ אָמֵן. Cong. אָמֵן

עֹשֶׂה שָׁלוֹם בִּמְרוֹמָיו הוּא בְּרַחֲמָיו יַעֲשֶׂה

שָׁלוֹם עָלֵינוּ וְעַל־כָּל־יִשְׂרָאֵל· וְאִמְרוּ אָמֵן ׃

Cong. אָמֵן   161

TRANSLITERATION OF THE SCHOLAR'S KADDISH
Ashkenazi pronunciation

Yisgaddal v'yiskaddash Sh'mey rabboh
B'olmoh dee-v'ro chir-usey,
V'yamlich malchusey
B'chay-yeychon uv'yo-mechon
Uvchay-yey de-chol beys yisro-eyl,
Ba-agoloh uvizman koreev;
V'imru omeyn.
Y'hey sh'mey rabboh m'vorach
L'olam ul'olmey olmah-yoh.
Yisborach v'yishtabach,
V'yispo-ar v'yisromam
V'yisnassey v'yis-haddar,
V'yis-alleh v'yis-hallal
Sh'mey de-kudshoh b'reech hu
L'eyloh min kol birchosoh v'shirosoh
Tush-b'chosoh v'nechemosoh
Daa-amiron b'olmoh;
V'imru omeyn.

Al yisro-eyl v'al rabbonon v'al talmeedeyhon v'al kol talmeedey salmeedey-hon v'al kol mon de-oskeen b'oraysoh dee b'ass-roh hoh-deyn v'dee b'chol assar va-assar. Y'hey l'hon ul'chon sh'lomoh rabboh chinoh v'chisdoh, v'rachamin v'chayin arichin um'zoney r'vichey ufurkonoh min kodom avuhon dee vishmah-yoh v'imru omeyn.

Y'hey sh'lomoh rabboh min sh'mah-yoh,
V'chay-yim tovim oleynu v'al kol yisro-eyl
V'imru omeyn.
O-seh sholom bimromov
Hu b'rachamov ya-aseh sholom
Oleynu v'al kol yisro-eyl
V'imru omeyn.

TRANSLITERATION OF THE SCHOLAR'S KADDISH
Sephardi pronunciation

Yitgaddal v'yitkaddash sh'meh rabbah
B'almah dee-v'ra chiru-teh
V'yamlich malchuteh
B'chay-yechon uv'yo-mechon
Uv'cha-yeh de-chol bet yisra-el
Ba-agalah uvizman kareev
V'imru Amen
Y'heh sh'mey rabbah m'varach
L'alam ul'almey almah-yah.
Yitbarach v'yishtabbach
V'yitpa-ar v'yitromam
V'yitnasseh v'yit-haddar
V'yit-alleh v'yit-hallal
Sh'mey de-kudshah b'reech hu
L'eylah min kol birchatah v'shiratah
Tush-b'chatah v'nechematah
Daa-ameeran b'almah
V'imru Amen

Al yisra-el v'al rabbanan v'al talmeedeh-hon v'al kol
talmeedeh talmeedeh-hon v'al kol man de-askin b'oraytah,
dee b'atrah ha-den v'dee b'chol atar va-atar
Y'heh l'hon ul'chon sh'lamah rabbah china v'chisdah
v'rachamin v'chayin arichin
Um'zoney r'vichey ufurkanah min kadam avuhon dee
vishmayah v'imru Amen
Y'hey sh'lamah rabbah min sh'mayah v'chay-yim tovim
alenu v'al kol yisra-el
V'imru Amen
O-seh shalom bimromav hu b'rachamav ya-ase shalom
alenu v'al kol yisra-el
V'imru Amen.

163

Mourners—May His great name be magnified and sanctified in the world that is to be created anew, where He will revive the dead, and raise them up into life eternal; will rebuild the city of Jerusalem, and establish His temple in the midst thereof; and will uproot all alien worship from the earth and restore the worship of the true God. O may the Holy One, blessed be He, reign in His sovereignty and glory during your life and during your days, and during the life of all the house of Israel, even speedily and at a near time, and say ye, Amen.

Congregation and Mourners—Let His great name be blessed for ever and to all eternity.

Mourners—Blessed, praised and glorified, exalted, extolled and honored, magnified and lauded be the name of the Holy One, blessed be He; though He be high above all blessings and hymns, praises and consolations, which are uttered in the world; and say ye, Amen.

Mourners—May there be abundant peace from heaven, and life for us and for all Israel; and say ye, Amen.

Mourners—He who maketh peace in His high places, may He make peace for us and for all Israel; and say ye, Amen.

THE BURIAL KADDISH

Mourners. יִתְגַּדַּל וְיִתְקַדַּשׁ שְׁמֵהּ רַבָּא בְּעָלְמָא

דִּי הוּא עָתִיד לְאִתְחַדָּתָא וּלְאַחֲיָאָה מֵתַיָּא

וּלְאַסָּקָא יָתְהוֹן לְחַיֵּי עָלְמָא. וּלְמִבְנֵא

קַרְתָּא דִי־יְרוּשְׁלֵם וּלְשַׁכְלֵל הֵיכְלֵהּ בְּגַוַּהּ.

וּלְמֶעֱקַר פָּלְחָנָא נֻכְרָאָה מֵאַרְעָא וְלַאֲתָבָא

פָּלְחָנָא דִי־שְׁמַיָּא לְאַתְרֵהּ. וְיַמְלַךְ קֻדְשָׁא

בְּרִיךְ הוּא בְּמַלְכוּתֵהּ וִיקָרֵהּ בְּחַיֵּיכוֹן

וּבְיוֹמֵיכוֹן וּבְחַיֵּי דִי־כָל־בֵּית יִשְׂרָאֵל

בַּעֲגָלָא וּבִזְמַן קָרִיב. וְאִמְרוּ אָמֵן:

Cong. יְהֵא שְׁמֵהּ רַבָּא מְבָרַךְ לְעָלַם וּלְעָלְמֵי
עָלְמַיָּא.

יִתְבָּרַךְ וְיִשְׁתַּבַּח וְיִתְפָּאַר וְיִתְרוֹמַם וְיִתְנַשֵּׂא וְיִתְהַדָּר

וְיִתְעַלֶּה וְיִתְהַלָּל שְׁמֵהּ דְּקֻדְשָׁא. *Cong.* בְּרִיךְ הוּא

(During the Ten Days of Pentinence, add: לְעֵלָּא (וּלְעֵלָּא

מִן כָּל־בִּרְכָתָא, וְשִׁירָתָא, תֻּשְׁבְּחָתָא, וְנֶחֱמָתָא

דַּאֲמִירָן בְּעָלְמָא. וְאִמְרוּ אָמֵן. *Cong.* אָמֵן

יְהֵא שְׁלָמָא רַבָּא מִן־שְׁמַיָּא וְחַיִּים עָלֵינוּ

וְעַל כָּל־יִשְׂרָאֵל. וְאִמְרוּ אָמֵן. *Cong.* אָמֵן

עוֹשֶׂה שָׁלוֹם בִּמְרוֹמָיו, הוּא יַעֲשֶׂה שָׁלוֹם

עָלֵינוּ. וְעַל כָּל־יִשְׂרָאֵל. וְאִמְרוּ אָמֵן. *Cong.* אָמֵן

165

TRANSLITERATION OF THE BURIAL KADDISH

Yisgaddal v'yiskaddash sh'mey rabboh
B'olmoh dee hu osid l'ischaddosoh ul'acha-yo-oh mey-
sayoh ul'assokoh yos-hon l'cha-yey olmoh. Ul'mivney kartoh
dee y'rushleym ul'shachleyl heych-ley b'gavah ul'meh-ekar
polchonoh nuchrohoh mey-ar-oh v'la-asovoh polchonoh
dee-sh'mayoh l'asrey v'yimlach kudshoh b'reech hu
b'malchoosey vee-korey

B'chay-yechon uv'yo-mechon
U'vcha-yey de-chol beys yisro-eyl
Ba-agoloh uvizman koreev
V'imru omeyn.
Yisborach v'yishtabbach
V'yispoar v'yisromam
V'yisnassey v'yis-haddar
V'yis-alleh v'yis-hallal
Sh'mey de-kudshoh b'reech hu
L'eyloh min kol birchosoh v'shirosoh
Tush-b 'chosoh v'nechemosoh
Daaameeron b'olmoh
V'imru omeyn.
Y'hey sh'lomoh rabboh min sh'mayoh
V'chay-yeem oleynu v'al kol yisro-el
V'imru omeyn.
O-seh sholom bimromov
Hu ya-aseh sholom
Oleynu v'al kol Yisro-eyl
V'imru omeyn.

A MEMORIAL PRAYER

אֵל מָלֵא רַחֲמִים שׁוֹכֵן בַּמְּרוֹמִים אֱלֹהַּ סְלִיחוֹת חַנּוּן
וְרַחוּם אֶרֶךְ אַפַּיִם וְרַב חֶסֶד. הַמְצֵא כַּפָּרַת פֶּשַׁע וְהַקְרֵבַת
יֶשַׁע וּמְנוּחָה נְכוֹנָה תַּחַת כַּנְפֵי הַשְּׁכִינָה בְּמַעֲלוֹת קְדוֹשִׁים
וּטְהוֹרִים כְּזֹהַר הָרָקִיעַ מַזְהִירִים. אֶת נִשְׁמַת
שֶׁהָלַךְ (שֶׁהָלְכָה) לְעוֹלָמוֹ (לְעוֹלָמָהּ): אָנָּא בַּעַל הָרַחֲמִים
זָכְרָה לוֹ (לָהּ) לְטוֹבָה כָּל זְכִיּוֹתָיו (זְכִיּוֹתֶיהָ) וְצִדְקוֹתָיו
(וְצִדְקוֹתֶיהָ) בְּאַרְצוֹת הַחַיִּים. וּפְתַח לוֹ (לָהּ) שַׁעֲרֵי צֶדֶק
וְאוֹרָה שַׁעֲרֵי חֶמְלָה וַחֲנִינָה. בְּסֵתֶר כְּנָפֶיךָ תַּסְתִּירֵהוּ
(תַּסְתִּירֶהָ) לְעוֹלָמִים. וּצְרוֹר בִּצְרוֹר הַחַיִּים אֶת נִשְׁמָתוֹ
(נִשְׁמָתָהּ). יְיָ הוּא נַחֲלָתוֹ (נַחֲלָתָהּ). וְיָנוּחַ (וְתָנוּחַ) בְּשָׁלוֹם
עַל מִשְׁכָּבוֹ (מִשְׁכָּבָהּ) וְנֹאמַר אָמֵן:

O Lord, who art full of compassion, who dwellest on high—God of forgiveness, who art merciful, slow to anger and abounding in lovingkindness, grant pardon of transgressions, nearness of salvation, and perfect rest beneath the shadow of Thy divine presence, in the exalted places among the holy and pure, who shine as the brightness of the firmament, to . . . who hath gone to his [her] eternal home. We beseech thee, O Lord of compassion, remember unto him [her] for good all the meritorious and pious deeds which he [she] wrought while on earth. Open unto him [her] the gates of righteousness and light, the gates of pity and grace. O shelter him [her] for evermore under the cover of thy wings; and let his [her] soul be bound up in the bond of eternal life. The Lord is his [her] inheritance; may he [she] rest in peace. And let us say, Amen.

IN MEMORY OF A FATHER

יִזְכּוֹר אֱלֹהִים נִשְׁמַת אָבִי מוֹרִי . . . [1] שֶׁהָלַךְ לְעוֹלָמוֹ,
בַּעֲבוּר שֶׁאֲנִי נוֹדֵר צְדָקָה בַּעֲדוֹ. בִּשְׂכַר זֶה תְּהֵא נַפְשׁוֹ
צְרוּרָה בִּצְרוֹר הַחַיִּים, עִם נִשְׁמַת אַבְרָהָם, יִצְחָק וְיַעֲקֹב,
שָׂרָה, רִבְקָה, רָחֵל וְלֵאָה, וְעִם שְׁאָר צַדִּיקִים וְצִדְקָנִיּוֹת שֶׁבְּגַן
עֵדֶן. וְנֹאמַר: אָמֵן!

May God remember the soul of my respected father . . . [1]
who has passed to his eternal rest. I pledge charity in his
behalf and pray that his soul be kept among the immortal
souls of Abraham, Isaac, Jacob, Sarah, Rebekah, Rachel,
Leah, and all the righteous men and women in paradise.
Amen.

Yizkor Elohim Nishmas ovee moree (name) sheh-holach
le'olomoh ba-avur sheh'anee nodeyr ts'dokoh ba-a-do
bischar zeh t-hey nafshow ts'ruroh bitsror hachayyim im
nishmos Avrohom, Yitschok, v'Ya-akov, Soroh, Rivkoh,
Rocheyl v'Leyoh v'im sh'or Tsaddikim v'tsiddkonneeyos
sheb'gan eyden, omeyn.

[1] The name of the deceased is supplied.

יִזְכּוֹר אֱלֹהִים נִשְׁמַת אִמִּי מוֹרָתִי . . . שֶׁהָלְכָה¹
לְעוֹלָמָהּ, בַּעֲבוּר שֶׁאֲנִי נוֹדֵר צְדָקָה בַּעֲדָהּ. בִּשְׂכַר זֶה תְּהֵא
נַפְשָׁהּ צְרוּרָה בִּצְרוֹר הַחַיִּים עִם נִשְׁמַת אַבְרָהָם, יִצְחָק
וְיַעֲקֹב, שָׂרָה, רִבְקָה, רָחֵל וְלֵאָה, וְעִם שְׁאָר צַדִּיקִים
וְצִדְקָנִיּוֹת שֶׁבְּגַן עֵדֶן. וְנֹאמַר: אָמֵן!

May God remember the soul of my respected mother . . .¹
who has passed to her eternal rest. I pledge charity in her
behalf and pray that her soul be kept among the immortal
souls of Abraham, Isaac, Jacob, Sarah, Rebekah, Rachel,
Leah, and all the righteous men and women in paradise.
Amen.

Yizkor Elohim nishmas imee morosee (name) sheh-holcho
le'olomoh ba-avur sheh'anee nodeyr ts'dokoh ba-a-doh
bischar zeh t-hey nafshoh ts'ruroh bitsror hachayyim im
nishmos Avrohom, Yitschok, v'Ya-akov, Soroh, Rivkoh,
Rocheyl v'Leyoh v'im sh'shr Tsaddikim v'tsiddkonees-yos
sheb'gan eyden, omeyn.

¹ The name of the deceased is supplied.

IN MEMORY OF A HUSBAND

יִזְכּוֹר אֱלֹהִים נִשְׁמַת בַּעְלִי הַיָּקָר . . .¹ שֶׁהָלַךְ לְעוֹלָמוֹ. בַּעֲבוּר שֶׁאֲנִי נוֹדֶרֶת צְדָקָה בַּעֲדוֹ, בִּשְׂכַר זֶה, תְּהֵא נַפְשׁוֹ צְרוּרָה בִּצְרוֹר הַחַיִּים עִם נִשְׁמוֹת אַבְרָהָם יִצְחָק וְיַעֲקֹב, שָׂרָה רִבְקָה רָחֵל וְלֵאָה, וְעִם שְׁאָר צַדִּיקִים וְצִדְקָנִיּוֹת שֶׁבְּגַן עֵדֶן. אָמֵן.

May God remember the soul of my beloved husband . . . ¹
who has passed to his eternal rest. I pledge charity in his
behalf and pray that his soul be kept among the immortal
souls of Abraham, Isaac, Jacob, Sarah, Rebekah, Rachel,
Leah, and all the righteous men and women in paradise.
Amen.

IN MEMORY OF A WIFE

יִזְכּוֹר אֱלֹהִים נִשְׁמַת אִשְׁתִּי הַיְקָרָה . . .¹ שֶׁהָלְכָה לְעוֹלָמָהּ. בַּעֲבוּר שֶׁאֲנִי נוֹדֵר צְדָקָה בַּעֲדָהּ, בִּשְׂכַר זֶה, תְּהֵא נַפְשָׁהּ צְרוּרָה בִּצְרוֹר הַחַיִּים עִם נִשְׁמוֹת אַבְרָהָם יִצְחָק וְיַעֲקֹב, שָׂרָה רִבְקָה רָחֵל וְלֵאָה, וְעִם שְׁאָר צַדִּיקִים וְצִדְקָנִיּוֹת שֶׁבְּגַן עֵדֶן. אָמֵן.

May God remember the soul of my beloved wife . . . ¹ who
has passed to her eternal rest. I pledge charity in her behalf
and pray that her soul be kept among the immortal souls of
Abraham, Isaac, Jacob, Sarah, Rebekah, Rachel, Leah,
and all the righteous men and women in paradise. Amen.

¹ The name of the deceased is supplied.

IN MEMORY OF A DAUGHTER

יִזְכּוֹר אֱלֹהִים נִשְׁמַת בִּתִּי . . . שֶׁהָלְכָה לְעוֹלָמָהּ. אָנָּא
תְּהִי נַפְשָׁהּ צְרוּרָה בִּצְרוֹר הַחַיִּים וּתְהִי מְנוּחָתָהּ כָּבוֹד שְׂבַע
שְׂמָחוֹת אֶת פָּנֶיךָ נְעִימוֹת בִּימִינְךָ נֶצַח. אָמֵן:

May God remember the soul of my beloved daughter who
hath gone to her repose. May her soul be bound up in the
bond of life. May her rest be glorious, with fulness of joy in
Thy presence, and bliss for evermore at Thy right hand.

IN MEMORY OF A SISTER

יִזְכּוֹר אֱלֹהִים נִשְׁמַת אֲחוֹתִי . . . בַּת . . . שֶׁהָלְכָה לְעוֹלָמָהּ.
אָנָּא תְּהִי נַפְשָׁהּ צְרוּרָה בִּצְרוֹר הַחַיִּים וּתְהִי מְנוּחָתָהּ כָּבוֹד
שְׂבַע שְׂמָחוֹת אֶת פָּנֶיךָ נְעִימוֹת בִּימִינְךָ נֶצַח. אָמֵן:

May God remember the soul of my beloved sister who
hath gone to her repose. May her soul be bound up in the
bond of life. May her rest be glorious, with fulness of joy in
Thy presence, and bliss for evermore at Thy right hand.

IN CASE OF A CHILD, READ THE FOLLOWING

אֵל מָלֵא רַחֲמִים שׁוֹכֵן בַּמְּרוֹמִים. הַמְצֵא מְנוּחָה נְכוֹנָה
תַּחַת כַּנְפֵי הַשְּׁכִינָה. בְּמַעֲלוֹת קְדוֹשִׁים וּטְהוֹרִים. כְּזֹהַר
הָרָקִיעַ מַזְהִירִים. אֶת־נִשְׁמַת הַיֶּלֶד (הַיַּלְדָה) _____
שֶׁהָלַךְ (שֶׁהָלְכָה) לְעוֹלָמוֹ (לְעוֹלָמָהּ). אָנָּא בַּעַל הָרַחֲמִים
הַסְתִּירֵהוּ (הַסְתִּירֶהָ) בְּסֵתֶר כְּנָפֶיךָ לְעוֹלָמִים. וּצְרוֹר
בִּצְרוֹר הַחַיִּים אֶת נִשְׁמָתוֹ (נִשְׁמָתָהּ). יְיָ הוּא נַחֲלָתוֹ
(נַחֲלָתָהּ) וְיָנוּחַ (וְתָנוּחַ) בְּשָׁלוֹם עַל מִשְׁכָּבוֹ (מִשְׁכָּבָהּ)
וְנֹאמַר אָמֵן:

O God, who art full of compassion, who dwellest on high,
grant perfect rest beneath the shadow of Thy divine presence,
in the exalted places among the holy and pure, who shine
as the brightness of the firmament, to the child . . . who hath
gone to his [her] eternal rest. We beseech thee, O Lord of
compassion, shelter his [her] soul for evermore under the
cover of thy wings. The Lord is his [her] portion. May he
[she] rest in peace. And let us say, Amen!

FOR THE VICTIMS OF NAZI PERSECUTION

אֵל מָלֵא רַחֲמִים שׁוֹכֵן בַּמְּרוֹמִים, הַמְצֵא מְנוּחָה נְכוֹנָה
תַּחַת כַּנְפֵי הַשְּׁכִינָה. בְּמַעֲלוֹת קְדוֹשִׁים וּטְהוֹרִים, כְּזֹהַר
הָרָקִיעַ מַזְהִירִים, אֶת נִשְׁמוֹת אַחֵינוּ אֲשֶׁר נִשְׂרְפוּ וְנֶהֶרְגוּ בִּידֵי
הַגֶּרְמָנִים הָאַכְזָרִים וְהָרוֹצְחִים, בָּאֲרָצוֹת תַּחַת מֶמְשֶׁלֶת
גֶּרְמַנְיָא. אָנָּא בַּעַל הָרַחֲמִים, הַסְתִּירֵם בְּסֵתֶר כְּנָפֶיךָ
לְעוֹלָמִים. וּצְרוֹר בִּצְרוֹר הַחַיִּים אֶת נִשְׁמָתָם. יְיָ הוּא
נַחֲלָתָם, וְיָנוּחוּ בְשָׁלוֹם עַל מִשְׁכָּבָם. וְנֹאמַר אָמֵן.

O God, Who art full of compassion, Who dwellest on high,
grant perfect rest beneath the shelter of Thy divine presence,
in the exalted places among the holy and pure who shine as
the brightness of the firmament, to our brethren whose
blood was spilt and who perished at the hands of the Nazi
oppressors in the countries of their domination. We beseech
Thee, Lord of Compassion, shelter them for evermore under
the cover of Thy wings, and let their souls be bound up in
the bond of eternal life. The Lord is their inheritance; may
they rest in peace. And let us say, Amen.

APPENDIX A

MEMORIAL RECORD	Name of Deceased (English)	Date of Death	Year	Month	Day	Name of Deceased (Hebrew)

GLOSSARY

Adar—The twelfth month of the Jewish calendar.

Aggadah—Ethical or homiletical portions of rabbinic literature.

Alav Hashalom—Lit. 'Peace be upon him.' A phrase used when the name of a departed is mentioned.

Aleha Hashalom—Lit. 'Peace be upon her.'

Alenu—Lit. 'It is our duty.' A prayer which is read at the end of all services.

Aliyah—Lit. 'Going up.' A term used when one is called up to the Reading of the Law.

Amidah—The name by which the prayer of the Eighteen Blessings (*Shemoneh Esrah*) is known. The term *Amidah* (Prayer said standing) is also known as *Tephillah*. It originally contained 18 Benedictions and now contains 19.

Amorah—Lit. 'Speaker', 'Interpreter'. The name given to the Rabbinic authorities responsible for the *Gemara*.

Aninut—The status of mourning between death and burial.

Aron—A coffin.

Ashkenazim—Jews of Germany and their descendants.

Av—The fifth month of the Jewish calendar.

Avelim—Mourners.

Bal Tashchit—Wanton destruction of property.

Bar-Mitzvah—Lit. 'Son of a Commandment.' A boy attaining thirteen years of age.

Beraita—Lit. 'Outside.' A Teaching of the *Tannaim* that has been excluded from the *Mishnah*.

Bet Din—Lit. 'House of Law' or 'judgment', a gathering of three or more learned men acting as a Jewish Court of Law.

Bet Hamidrash—House of Study.

Bet Olam—Lit. 'Eternal House' i.e. a cemetery.

Bikkur Cholim—Visiting the sick.

Brit—Lit. 'Covenant,' circumcision ceremony.

Cabbalah—Jewish Mysticism.

Chanukah—Lit. 'Dedication.' The Festival is celebrated for eight days from the 25th of *Kislev*.

Chassidim—Pietists, followers of Rabbi Israel Baal Shem *Tov* (1700–1760).

Chevrah Kadisha—Lit. 'Holy Brotherhood.' A society the members of which look after the burial and the rites connected with it.

Chodesh—Month.

Chol Hamoed—The half festive days or the secular days of Passover and *Sukkot*.

Chukat Hagoy—Aping the ways of the Gentiles.

Cohen—A Priest, a descendant of Aaron (v. Lev. XXI, XXII).

Dibbuk—A soul of a sinner which attaches itself to a living body.

Din—Law.

El Male Rachamim—Lit. 'God full of compassion.' A memorial Prayer.

Elul—Sixth month of the Jewish calendar.

Eretz Israel—The land of Israel.

Etrog—A citron. One of the 'four kinds of plants' used during the festival of *Sukkot*.

Gan Eden—Garden of Eden, Paradise.

Gaon, pl. *Geonim*—The title of the head of the Rabbinical Academies in Babylon.

Gehinnom—Hell, the Valley of Hinnom.

Gilgul—Transmigration of a soul.

Gosess—A dying person.

Haftarah—Lit. 'Conclusion,' concluding the Reading of the Torah with a passage from the Prophets.

Haggadah—Lit. 'telling.' The *Haggadah* is the book which tells the story of the Exodus from Egypt.

Hakkafot—Lit. Circuits. Processions with the Torah around the *Bima* on *Simchat Torah*.

Halachah, pl. *Halachot*—Lit. 'Guidance.' The law or the legal literature of the Jews.

Hallel—Hymns of praise consisting of six Psalms and recited on certain festive days of the year.

Halvayat Hamet—Attending a funeral.

Hashkavah—Memorial prayer among the Sephardim corresponding to the Ashkenazi prayer of El Male Rachamim.

Havdalah—Lit. 'Division.' The benedictions recited at the termination of the Sabbath and festivals.

Hazkarat Neshamot—Memorial Services.

Hesped—Eulogy.

Kaddish, pl. *Kaddishim*—Lit. 'Holy' or 'sacred' and refers to the doxology recited in the Synagogue.

Kavod Lamet—Honouring the dead.

Keriah—Rending of the garment.

Kiddush Hashem—Sanctification of God's Name.

Kinot—Lamentations recited on the ninth day of *Av*.

Lag B'Omer—The thirty-third day of the *Omer* corresponding to the 18th of *Iyar*, The Scholar's Feast.

Lechah Dodi—Lit. 'Come my beloved.' A hymn sung during the Friday eve Service.

Leshon Ha Kodesh—The Holy Tongue, Hebrew.

Maariv—Evening Service.

Maftir—Concluding. The last portion of the *Sidrah* is known as *Maftir*.

Masorah—The body of tradition which concerns itself with the correct spelling, writing and reading of the Hebrew Bible.

Matzah—Unleavened bread.

Matzevah—Tombstone.

Menachem Avel—Comforting the mourner.

Megillah—Lit. 'Scroll,' a term commonly applied to the Book of Esther.

Met Mitzvah—A corpse lying unattended with nobody to arrange for its burial. The duty of burying it devolves upon whomsoever discovers it even if he be a High Priest.

Midrash, pl. *Midrashim*—Lit. 'expositions'. The books devoted to the homiletic exposition of the Scriptures.

Minchah—Afternoon Service.

Minhag—custom, rite.

Minyan—Lit. 'Number,' or quorum. Ten men above the age of thirteen.

Mishnah—Lit. 'Repetition.' The collection of the statements of the *Tannaim* edited by Rabbi Judah the Patriarch 135–220.

Mitnagged—Lit. Opponent. Those who opposed *Chassidism*.

Mohel—Circumciser.

Musaph—Additional prayers on Sabbath, Holidays and *Rosh Chodesh*.

Nasi—Lit. 'Prince.'

Nisan—The first month of the Jewish calender.

Olam Haba—The World to Come.

Omer—'Sheaf.' The seven weeks counted between Passover and Pentecost.

Onen—A mourner while his dead relatives are awaiting burial.

Passover—The Festival commemorating the liberation of the Jews from their bondage in Egypt. The festival is kept for eight days, from the 15th of *Nisan* to the 22nd.

Pidyon Haben—Redemption of the first-born son is a ceremony held on the thirty-first day of birth.

Piyyutim—Liturgical poetry for sabbaths and the holidays.

Purim—Lit. 'Lots.' The festival is celebrated on the 14th of *Adar* in commemoration of the deliverance of the Jews in Persia from the hands of Haman.

Rashi—Abbreviation of Rabbi Solomon b. Isaac (1040–1105), the great commentator of the Bible and Talmud.

Responsa—Written replies given to questions (*Teshuvot*) on all aspects of Jewish Law by qualified authorities from the time of the late *Geonim* to the present day.

Rosh Chodesh—New Moon.

Rosh Hashanah—New Year, the 1st and 2nd days of *Tishri*.

Sabbath *Hagadol*—Lit. 'The Great Sabbath.' The Sabbath preceding Passover.

Sandek—The one who holds the baby on his knees during the Circumcision.

Seder—Lit. 'Order.' The order of the home service on Passover.

Selichot—Penitential Prayers.

Shalach Manot—The sending of gifts on the day of *Purim*.

Shalosh Seudot—The Third Meal commences after *Minchah* and lasts until the end of the Sabbath. 'They shall recite the Afternoon prayer,' says Maimonides, and 'commence the Third Meal and eat and drink until the expiry of the Sabbath.'

Shavuot—Pentecost or the Feast of Weeks celebrated on the 6th and 7th of *Sivan*.

Shechinah—The Divine Presence.

Shehecheyanu—Lit. 'Who has kept us alive'. A benediction pronounced on occasions of importance.

Shemini Atzeret—The Feast of the Eight day or the Eight Day of Solemn Assembly.

Sheol—The nether world of the grave.

Shivah—Lit. 'Seven' and refers to the seven days of mourning.

Shophar—A ram's horn used in the services of New Year and at the conclusion of the Day of Atonement.

Shulchan Aruch—Lit. 'Table Prepared.' A Code of Jewish Law by Rabbi Joseph Caro (1488–1575).

Siddur—The authorised daily prayer book of the Jews.

Simchah—A joyous occasion.

Simchat Torah—Rejoicing of the Law, the festival immediately after *Sukkot*.

Sivan—Ninth month of the Jewish calendar.

Siyyum—Lit. 'Completion.' When a course of study is completed the occasion is marked by a celebration.

Sukkah—The festive booth for Tabernacles (Lev. XXIII: 34).

Sukkot—The festival commemorates the wandering of the

children of Israel in the wilderness and is observed from
the 15th to the 23rd of *Tishri*.

Tabernacles, see Sukkot.

Tachanun—Supplicatory prayers, recited at morning and
afternoon services.

Tachrichim—Shrouds of the dead.

Taharah—The ritual of cleansing a corpse.

Tallit—The prayer-shawl.

Talmud—The general sense of the word is study of the Law.
It is more common in the narrow sense of the comments
and the discussions (*Gemara*) on the text of the *Mishnah*
by the Palestinian and Babylonian scholars from the
third to the fifth centuries C.E. which constitute the
Palestinian Talmud and the Babylonian Talmud.

The Babylonian Talmud (*Bavli*) contains nearly 3,000
pages and was edited by Rav Ashi (352–427), whereas
the Palestinian Talmud (*Yerushalmi*) was finished in the
fifth century and is only one seventh as long as the
Babylonian Talmud.

Tammuz—The fourth month of the Jewish calendar.

Tanna—A teacher quoted in the *Mishnah* or *Beraita*.

Targum—Aramaic translation of the Bible.

Techinah—Supplication. A supplementary devotional
prayer in Yiddish.

Tephillin—Phylacteries; small cases containing passages
from the Scriptures and affixed to the forehead and arm
during the recital of morning prayers (Deut. VI: 8).

Tevet—Tenth month of the Jewish calendar.

Tisha B'Av—The Fast of the 9th of *Av* commemorates the
destruction of both the First and the Second Temples
(586 B.C.E. and 70 C.E.).

Tishri—The seventh month of the Jewish calendar.

Torah—Lit. 'Teaching.' The whole body of Jewish religious
literature.

Tosaphot—Critical glosses on the Talmud by French Rabbis
of the twelfth and thirteenth centuries.

Vidduy—Confession.

Yahrzeit—Anniversary of death.

Yom Kippur—The Day of Atonement.

Yom Tov—'A good day,' generally applied to Festivals.

Zaddik—A righteous man.

Zecher Zaddik Livrachah—'May the memory of the Righteous be for a blessing.'

Zechut Avot—The Merit of the Fathers.

Zedakah—Righteousness, charity.

Zidduk Hadin—'Acknowledgement of the Divine Judgment.' Part of the Burial Service.

Zizit—The Biblical name of the fringes which are attached to each of the four corners of the garment (Num. XIV: 38).

Zohar—Title of the mystical work introduced into Spain by Moses da Leon at the end of the 13th century and attributed to Rabbi Simeon bar Yochai.

Zuz—Silver coin, one fourth of a Shekel.

BIBLIOGRAPHY

GREENWALD, RABBI LEOPOLD, *Kol Bo Al Avelut* (On Laws of Mourning), 3 Vols. (New York, 1947–51).

HIGGER, DR MICHAEL, *Semachot and Semachot of R. Hiyya.* (New York, 1931).

Maimonides, *Mishneh Torah Hilchot Evel.* (New York, 1947).

Nachmanides *Torat ha-Adam.* (Warsaw, 1841).

Shulchan Aruch, Yoreh Deah 335–403. Tran. Chaim N. Denburg. (Montreal, 1954).

TUKECHINSKY, YECHIEL M., *Gesher ha-Chayyim.* 2 Vols. (Jerusalem, 1944).

INDEX